Truth AND Reconciliation

IN CANADIAN SCHOOLS

Truth AND Reconciliation
IN CANADIAN SCHOOLS

Pamela Rose Toulouse

PORTAGE &
MAIN PRESS

Portage & Main Press gratefully acknowledges the financial support of the Province of Manitoba through the Department of Sport, Culture & Heritage and the Manitoba Book Publishing Tax Credit, and the Government of Canada through the Canada Book Fund (CBF) for our publishing activities.

Printed and bound in Canada by Friesens
Design by Relish New Brand Experience
Black and white illustrations by Jess Dixon

Library and Archives Canada Cataloguing in Publication

Toulouse, Pamela Rose, author

Truth and reconciliation in Canadian schools / Pamela Rose Toulouse.

Issued in print and electronic formats.

ISBN 978-1-55379-745-6 (softcover).--ISBN 978-1-55379-746-3 (EPUB)

1. Native peoples--Study and teaching--Canada. I. Title.

E96.2.T68 2018   371.829'97071   C2017-906341-3

C2017-906342-1

21 20 19 18   1 2 3 4 5

PORTAGE & MAIN PRESS

1-800-667-9673
www.portageandmainpress.com
Winnipeg, Manitoba
Treaty 1 Territory and homeland of the Métis Nation.

Contents

Acknowledgments

I wish to take this opportunity to remember the more than one hundred and fifty thousand Indigenous children who attended residential schools. My grandmother was one of those children, and this book is a deeply personal one because of her. She survived and became one of the greatest influences in my life. She taught me to laugh, right from the belly and right from the heart.

It is important that I say *Chi Meegwetch* – "thank you" in Anishinaabemowin (Ojibwe) – to several individuals and groups for making this book, *Truth and Reconciliation in Canadian Schools*, possible.

On the professional front:

At Portage & Main Press, I would like to recognize Annalee Greenberg, Patricia Robertson, and Leigh Hambly for being such wonderful supporters (and editors).

To Laurentian University, my workplace, for providing me with an environment and the space to research and publish.

To the devoted Indigenous leaders and educators across this country who are working toward making our schools (and world) a better place for our kids.

On the personal front:

To my parents, Nelson Toulouse and Dorothy Toulouse (née Recollet – in the Spirit World), thank you for teaching me the values of leadership, dedication, and kindness.

To my husband, Luc Watier, your positive outlook on the world and your care of our little fur-family makes me happy and complete every day.

To my siblings, their spouses, and my nephews/nieces, our get-togethers continue to leave me with lots of awesome memories and tons of good laughs.

Preface

In 2015, the Truth and Reconciliation Commission of Canada (TRC) released its final report, complete with 94 Calls to Action that included action on education for reconciliation. The voices of Indigenous children who attended residential schools became the guiding light for me in the entire process of writing this book. I wondered what my grandmother, Madonna Rose Toulouse, who had journeyed to the Spirit World the year before, would think and say about the TRC process. She attended the infamous St. Joseph's Residential School for girls in Spanish, Ontario, and nearly died there. I had the opportunity to hear many of her stories (often painful and often funny) of the time she spent at Spanish. That really became the inspirational force that connected me to the TRC and the Calls to Action on education for reconciliation. I knew that I had to do my part and take the gifts that the Creator had given me and do something in response to those Calls. My grandmother always had a very strong work ethic and this provided me with the perseverance to write this book.

There are many authentic and deeply meaningful resources on residential schools being developed across this land. There are also equally abundant anthologies on treaties, Indigenous histories, and First Nation/Métis/Inuit perspectives. The one area where I do see a need is for a resource for elementary and secondary teachers that captures the preceding topics in an accessible manner. This book, *Truth and Reconciliation in Canadian Schools*, does so by providing informative chapters (with current data, facts, insights, resources, curriculum tables, and teaching strategies) followed by K to 12 lesson plans that are ready for immediate implementation. This book has become my way to give back to the many communities that require this text and are looking for a guide to building relationships with social action at their core.

What is truth? What is reconciliation? It is a personal look at what we know, what we don't know, and what we need to do to move forward respectfully. It means we go beyond guilt, shame, and anger to create educational spaces where our children and youth can grow together as healthy citizens. Truth and reconciliation in a Canadian school context requires educators, administrators, and organizations that work diligently at ensuring all students and communities thrive. It involves a lot of humility and risk-taking in pushing the boundaries of learning by making initiatives in human (and other-than-human) rights foundational to the school year. Truth and reconciliation is even more necessary in a world that is challenged and for our children and youth who have inherited it.

In conclusion, I thank you, the reader, for taking this journey with me. The effects of your work in helping to implement education for reconciliation are and will be intergenerational.

"Take what you need from this book, change it, leave what you don't need, and pass it on."

Introduction

WHO THIS BOOK IS FOR

Every province and territory across this land has been challenged to respond to the 94 Calls to Action from the 2015 final report of the Truth and Reconciliation Commission of Canada (TRC). Each government department or ministry committed to education has a unique opportunity to implement those calls that are relevant to teaching and learning in a meaningful way for all students. *Truth and Reconciliation in Canadian Schools* has been written for educators looking for a hands-on resource that offers ways to incorporate those calls that are specific to elementary and secondary classrooms. It is designed to be teacher-friendly and is written in accessible language.

HOW TO USE THIS BOOK

Truth and Reconciliation in Canadian Schools is divided into two sections. Part 1: Program Foundations, provides the necessary background on the topics emerging from those Calls to Action on education for reconciliation in the TRC final report. Part 2: Truth and Reconciliation Lesson Plans by Grade, offers lesson plans for K to 12 that translate those topics into practical teaching and learning strategies for the classroom.

Each of the five chapters in Part 1: Program Foundations, includes the Call to Action it will address, curriculum tables, current facts, strategies, resources, and the personal connection of the author to the themes. These chapters also include the following:

- the legacy of residential schools (information, timeline, photographs, insights)
- the Indigenous peoples of Canada (statistics, value differences, effects of acts/legislation)
- treaties of Canada (differing views, summary of treaties, oral/written histories)
- contributions of Indigenous peoples (by geography, by First Nations, Turtle Island map)
- sacred circle teachings (detailed descriptions, seven living philosophies, Indigenous games)

Part 2: Truth and Reconciliation Lesson Plans by Grade, includes a number of lesson plans that can be implemented (or adapted) immediately. They are each organized by suggested scope and sequence according to content and student development. They take a holistic approach that includes the spiritual, physical, emotional, and intellectual aspects of learning. All lessons contain the following:

- background information, key terms, and the Indigenous concept to be shared (e.g., teaching, historical fact, traditional use, contemporary story)

- time needed, materials/resources (including a reproducible master), and considerations and cautions
- step-by-step plans with learning goals
- strategies for engagement and consolidation questions
- assessment for, as, and of learning; curricular extensions; and potential adaptations

PART 1

Program Foundations

Introduction to
PART 1: Program Foundations

The chapters that follow offer elementary and secondary teachers information, illustrations, insights, facts, resources, and strategies that honour Indigenous history and worldview. The knowledge and pedagogy being discussed in this guide for implementation in schools is relevant for all learners, especially in educational spaces that embrace the Calls to Action from the Truth and Reconciliation Commission of Canada final report.

Chapter 1. Residential Schools Legacy provides an overview of

- education in traditional societies
- a timeline of key events in residential schools
- an image journey of life at residential school
- why literacy is an ideal approach to teaching about residential schools
- K to 12 literacy curriculum table with resources on residential schools
- reconciliation activities with Project of Heart

Chapter 2. Indigenous Peoples of Canada provides an overview of

- the population of Indigenous peoples by province and territory
- traditional Indigenous values vs. technological society values
- the Indian Act of 1876
- personal perspectives on First Nation, Inuit, and Métis peoples
- why the arts is an ideal approach to teaching about Indigenous peoples of Canada
- K to 12 arts curriculum table with resources on Indigenous peoples

Chapter 3. Treaties of Canada provides an overview of

- differing views on treaties
- summaries of select treaties and relevant acts
- treaty, land, and culture resources by province and territory
- wampum belts, sacred scrolls, artifacts, and oral history
- why social studies, history, geography, Canadian studies, and world studies are ideal approaches to teaching about treaties
- curriculum table for K to 12 social studies, history, geography, Canadian studies, and world studies with resources on Indigenous treaties

Chapter 4. Contributions of Indigenous Peoples provides an overview of

- Turtle Island and Indigenous traditional lands
- Indigenous contributions by geographic area
- specific contributions of First Nation, Inuit, and Métis peoples
- Anishinaabek, Mushkegowuk, and Haudenosaunee contributions
- why science is an ideal approach to teaching about Indigenous contributions
- K to 12 science curriculum table with resources on Indigenous contributions

Chapter 5. Sacred Circle Teachings provides an overview of

- the teachings of the sacred circle
- teachings from the east with the three moons of spring
- teachings from the south with the three moons of summer
- teachings from the west with the three moons of fall
- teachings from the north with the four moons of winter
- seven living teachings
- why health and physical education is an ideal approach to teaching about the sacred circle
- K to 12 health and physical education curriculum table with Indigenous resources
- integrating Indigenous games into schools

CHAPTER 1. Residential Schools Legacy

Call 63.i. – Education for Reconciliation (TRC Calls to Action)
"We call upon the Council of Ministers of Education, Canada to maintain an annual commitment to Aboriginal education issues, including ... implementing Kindergarten to Grade Twelve curriculum and learning resources on ... the history and legacy of residential schools."

INTRODUCTION

My grandmother Madonna Rose Toulouse attended St. Joseph's Residential School for girls in Spanish, Ontario, when she was a child. She nearly died there from complications associated with pneumonia. I remember her telling me about this experience. She recalled how the priest came in and gave her the last rites (M. Toulouse, personal communication, April 15, 2011). Other girls had gathered around her and told her "she was going to die" (ibid.). My grandmother was always a fighter and, even as a child confronting death, she faced this illness head-on. After she recovered, the authorities at the school decided to send her back home to her family in Wikwemikong (Manitoulin Island, Ontario).

For the rest of her time in this world, she suffered with chronic lung issues from internal scarring as a result of this illness. She never complained, and I can definitely say that she lived a full life. My grandmother was one of the most resilient, hard-working, stubborn, and funny women I have ever known. I was so lucky to be her granddaughter.

One hundred percent of Indigenous peoples have been affected by the legacy of residential schools in some way, whether through loss of culture, loss of language, dislocation from families and communities, and/or being the subjects of racism (Historica Canada n.d.; Truth and Reconciliation Commission of Canada 2015). For some – and for far too many – these life-altering events manifested as long-term diseases best described as dysfunction, addiction, and/or chronic illness (First Nations Education Steering Committee & First Nations Schools Association 2015). Each Indigenous family in Canada has a story to tell about the effects of residential schools and colonial history in their lives. The story of my grandmother and our family is at the same time painfully unique and altogether common. Our shared experiences of life, death, loss, hope, sadness, and happiness are among the many living stories revealed through the Truth and Reconciliation Commission of Canada (TRC) process. On June 3, 2015, when the TRC released its final report, I sat in my home relieved that the truth of what really happened to Indigenous children here in Canada was finally being heard. I am sure my grandmother Madonna Rose Toulouse, already in the Spirit World, was thankful for this as well.

Figure 1.1. Map of residential schools in Canada.

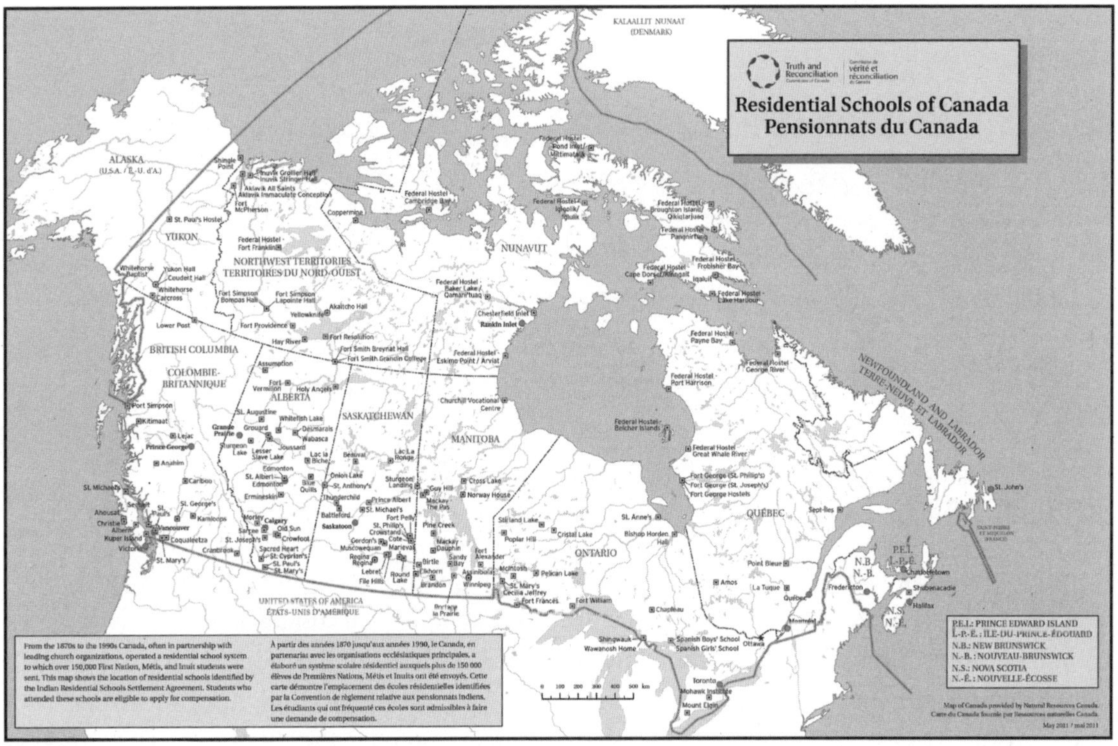

The Calls to Action in the TRC final report provide practical recommendations to begin addressing the inequities and suffering that Indigenous communities have endured. For me, education for reconciliation and "implementing Kindergarten to Grade Twelve curriculum and learning resources on … the history and legacy of residential schools" (TRC, 331) is paramount. This chapter therefore embraces that Call to Action and provides a space for this living narrative about residential schooling to be told.

As we begin our journey together, I ask you, the reader, to reflect on the following facts:

- The first residential school (called a boarding school at the time) was built near Quebec City in the early 17th century. Indigenous parents would not send their children there, and most students ran away once admitted (TRC 2015).

- The model for residential schools came from European reformatories and American industrial schools. These were designed for children who were poor, abandoned, or neglected. Most of these places were already known for their violence (ibid.).

- In 1907, Indian Affairs Chief Medical Officer Dr. P.H. Bryce reported that 15 to 25 percent of Aboriginal children (and up to 40 percent in some locations) were dying in residential schools. After he was forced to retire in 1922, he published *The Story of a National Crime: Being a Record of the Health Conditions of the Indians of Canada from*

1904 to 1921 (Government of Northwest Territories, Government of Nunavut & Legacy of Hope Foundation 2013).

- Between 1831 and 1996, 132 residential schools were in operation in Canada with 150 000 First Nation, Métis, and Inuit children enrolled (ibid.).

EDUCATION IN TRADITIONAL INDIGENOUS SOCIETIES

Education in traditional Indigenous societies focused on the whole person. The physical, emotional, intellectual, and spiritual needs of each person were the foundation for learning. The teaching of children was a communal responsibility, and educators came in many forms (e.g., human, spirit, land, animals). Indigenous pedagogy combined focused observation, hands-on activities, risk-taking, reflection, and problem-solving (Alberta Aboriginal Services Branch & Learning and Teaching Resources Branch 2005). Children and youth were encouraged to be creative, and their education helped to develop the capacity of their communities.

For example, in my nation, the Anishinaabe, we have *dodems* (clans) that are aligned with specific roles. I belong to the Fish Clan (*Ginoozhe indoodem*), and we are entrusted to be the educators, philosophers, and mediators. Learning about our own gifts is the first step in this form of learning (Toulouse 2016a). We develop those gifts (e.g., skills, knowledge, values, traits) in order to be our best selves. These gifts are then integrated into the collective work of our dodems. For example, my gift of humour has been essential to my role as a compassionate teacher. Our dodems are thus part of a larger whole whereby the First Nation survives and thrives based upon the quality and authenticity of this traditional education system.

The concept that learning is lifelong continues to resonate with Indigenous peoples today. Traditional societies embraced this idea by reinforcing the notion that we all come from communities of learners (Alberta Aboriginal Services Branch & Learning and Teaching Resources Branch 2005). Education is on a birth-to-death continuum; knowledge is never-ending and evolving. Traditional education, because it provided a space for mystery and curiosity to be ever-present, was unique. It was okay not to have answers for everything. It was okay to question and not always be in search of solutions.

For example, we Anishinaabe understand that the Creator (*Gchi-Manitou*) is the Great Mystery and is beyond human comprehension (Benton-Banai 2008). We also understand from our teachings that all Creation stories are true (ibid.). This perspective allows for equality to exist and means that our way of thinking is one of reflection and growth. We don't have the need to argue that our way is the only way. Instead, we respect that there are multiple paths and journeys in this world that we occupy together.

Traditional Indigenous education collided with non-Indigenous forms of education because they are complete opposites. Non-Indigenous forms of education introduced in North America were embedded with beliefs about superiority/inferiority, expert/non-expert, living/dead, and civilized/savage (Deloria 2003). Indigenous peoples were then labelled by these non-Indigenous systems as less-than, uncivilized, and non-human. This Eurocentric worldview paved the way for residential schools to become a reality (First Nations Education Steering Committee &

First Nations Schools Association 2015). It is an example of how a worldview, combined with power, can adversely affect entire generations of Indigenous peoples (Government of Northwest Territories et al. 2013). These beliefs resulted in 150 000 Indigenous children being forcibly taken from their homes and subjected to an education that was oftentimes abusive (TRC 2015).

What did the progression of residential schools look like? How did it evolve? Table 1.1 provides a timeline of events from the origin of residential schools in Canada to present day.

Table 1.1. Residential School Timeline

DATE	EVENT
17th century	First Indigenous boarding school opens near Quebec City (Roman Catholic).
1820s	Boarding school, mainly for Métis children, opens at Red River, Manitoba (Anglican).
1834–1970	Mohawk Institute (mission school) on the Grand River in Ontario is in operation.
1847	Egerton Ryerson, superintendent of schools for Upper Canada, recommends that residential schools be established for Indigenous peoples with a focus on agricultural techniques (based upon similar recommendations from the Bagot Commission of 1842–44).
1879	The Davin Report, commissioned by Sir John A. Macdonald to study the effectiveness of industrial boarding schools in the United States, is released. It recommends that Indian industrial schools are needed in Canada and that separating the children from their parents is critical to assimilation.
1883	Sir John A. Macdonald accepts the recommendations of the Davin Report and approves the construction of Indian residential schools in the West.
1889	Allegations of physical and sexual abuse against Indigenous children are reported at Rupert's Land Residential School (Manitoba).
1892	Churches and the federal government enter into a formal agreement to operate residential schools. The focus is on assimilation and religion.
1920	Duncan Campbell Scott, Deputy Superintendent General of Indian Affairs, makes it compulsory for Indigenous children between 7 and 15 years of age to attend residential schools.
1940	Provincial curriculum standards are implemented in residential schools by the federal government.
1950	Indian Affairs reports that 40 percent of teaching staff at residential schools have no training, and that Indigenous children spend most of their day doing manual labour.
1958	Regional inspectors from Indian Affairs recommend the closing of residential schools.
1969	The federal government takes over the residential schools and ends its formal relationship with the churches.
1996	The last residential school closes in Punnichy, Saskatchewan (Gordon Indian Residential School).
1998	The Aboriginal Healing Foundation is created with an 11-year mandate to administer $350 million for projects that address the trauma of residential school survivors, their families, and their communities.

Truth and Reconciliation in Canadian Schools

DATE	EVENT
2005	National Chief Phil Fontaine of the Assembly of First Nations announces that a class-action lawsuit against the Government of Canada over residential school abuse is being launched.
2007	The Indian Residential Schools Settlement Agreement – the result of the class-action lawsuit – is implemented to redress survivor claims of abuse.
2008	In June, Prime Minister Stephen Harper, on behalf of the Government of Canada, apologizes for its role in the abuses against Indigenous peoples at residential schools.
2008	The Truth and Reconciliation Commission of Canada is established to document the truth of survivors, families, and communities in order to inform all Canadians about what happened in Indian residential schools, and to begin a process of understanding and healing between Canadians and Indigenous communities.

This timeline focuses on residential schools only and does not include colonial policies affecting Indigenous peoples during this period. (TRC 2015; Legacy of Hope Foundation 2017)

A HISTORY OF RESIDENTIAL SCHOOLS IN PHOTOGRAPHS

Daily life in residential schools was regimented and is best described as "the drudgery of doing the chores necessary to make the schools self-sustaining" (TRC 2015, 4). Several reports document the farming out of Indigenous children as labourers and domestic help for private homes and businesses. The education of Indigenous children was not only limited, but also did not consider the traditional knowledge they possessed as a form of education. In fact, many of the lessons promoted a self-destructive view of Indigenous cultures. We became one-dimensional caricatures in the media and in the eyes of non-Indigenous citizens. Disturbingly, Indigenous students, separated from their communities, began to internalize these images of themselves, as well.

Although my grandmother nearly died at the residential school she attended in Spanish, Ontario, she was also able to talk about positive experiences during her stay there. Many survivors have relayed similar stories about the skills, tools, and friendships acquired in the schools (First Nations Education Steering Committee & First Nations Schools Association 2015; TRC 2015). My grandmother learned how to read and became very devoted to the Catholic faith. She mastered sewing and also learned about agriculture and farming, knowledge she applied her entire life, being known for her abundant gardens. She never lost her Anishinaabemowin language and was an avid speaker of it.

Her education, as for many others in residential school, was organized by gender-appointed tasks. The girls had their specific training (see figure 1.2) and the boys had theirs. Basil Johnston, in his book *Indian School Days* (1988, 34), recalls a day in a boy's education at Spanish. "From every part of the institution and the grounds boys scurried back to the recreation hall with their equipment. 8:55 AM Clang! Clang! Clang! Line up again. According to the system then in operation half the senior boys went to class, while the other half went to work not only to practise a trade but also to provide the labour needed to run the institution."

Figure 1.2. Shubenacadie Indian Residential School in Nova Scotia, 1929

Mi'kmaq girls at their sewing class, led by one of the nuns.

The days in residential schools were consumed with work of some type. The nights were spent in dormitories (see figure 1.3) with their row upon row of beds. My grandmother often said that what she remembered most about her sleeping quarters at the school, where her wool blanket did not cover her, was the cold. Many of the young girls complained about the cold and dampness, especially during fire drills. They all had to get up, no matter the conditions, form into lines, and head outside. The freezing temperatures, both inside and out, were what my grandmother talked about the most.

I always appreciated how she took those experiences and turned them into a lesson (albeit sometimes harsh) about being thankful. She would discuss the cold at residential school and turn that into a springboard to share a memory about the warmth of her parents' cabin on Rabbit Island in Wikwemikong (Manitoulin Island, Ontario). She talked about that cabin, the smell of the wood fire, the homemade food, the Anishinaabemowin language, her family, and the laughter that was present. Her descriptions of the rolling hills, playing with her siblings, eating her grandmother's preserves, and the sharing of stories at night had me missing a place I had never been to. It always amazed me how my grandmother could take a story of survival to a place of reconciliation within herself.

Figure 1.3. Boys' dormitory, Cross Lake Indian Residential School, Manitoba, 1940

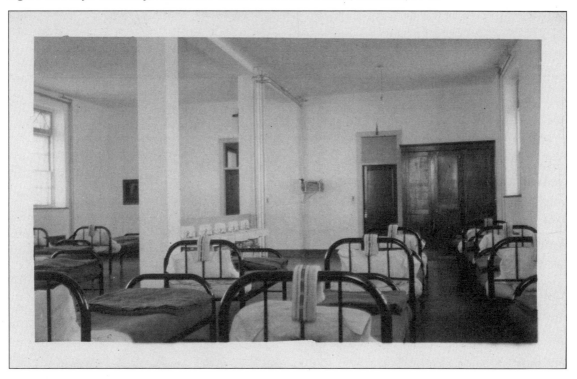

Typical sleeping arrangements for boys in residential schools.

The residential school campaign in Canada left no area of the country untouched. In the north, where education was modelled on the residential schools operating in southern Canada, hostels were set up for Inuit children, using tents to house smaller groups of Indigenous students (Government of Northwest Territories et al. 2013). Most northern residential schools used this tent system as a cheaper way to enroll more Indigenous children because the cost of building in northern conditions was astronomical. Although the system of residential schools came to Canada's north later, it had the highest number of students in attendance. For example, 50 percent of Indigenous peoples in the Yukon and Northwest Territories over the age of 61 have attended a residential school (ibid.). This alarming figure shows the extent of the schools' harmful effects on northern First Nations. Children of Métis families in the north were also placed in these schools, and Métis peoples nearly had their distinct Michif language – a blend of French, Cree, and Ojibwe – completely decimated throughout Canada (see figure 1.4). The power of residential schools and the intergenerational damage they inflicted on Inuit and Métis communities are immense. Today's Inuit youth have the highest suicide rate in the world (Inuit Tapiriit Kanatami 2016).

Teaching about residential schools is necessary. It is one of the key ways in which we can all move forward together as a country. Non-Indigenous Canadians have the right to know both about the effects of these schools and how we can heal in a truthful and meaningful way. I believe that the development of curriculum about residential schools – a TRC Call to Action – requires a specific pedagogical approach, including literacy methods, reconciliation activities, and planned relationship-building with Indigenous communities.

Two Métis girls and one Inuit girl at school.

WHY LITERACY IS AN IDEAL APPROACH TO TEACHING ABOUT RESIDENTIAL SCHOOLS

Fear and discomfort are the reasons educators cite most in their reluctance to teach Indigenous culture and history (Dion 2014; St. Denis 2010). Most teachers want to get it right and honour the knowledge of Indigenous peoples, but are concerned about the sensitive nature of the topic of residential schools and their effects. Having the appropriate resources and training to respond to the Call to Action and teach this topic in K to 12 is critical.

Although I am not a survivor of a residential school, I am a person who has experienced the intergenerational effects. This Call to Action would benefit from implementing a literacy approach by harnessing the power of story. It can transform the listener, reader, or viewer and connect them to the lives of these survivors by building a bridge that transcends history and time.

I believe the voices of residential-school survivors are fundamental in guiding the way by telling their stories.

Table 1.2 is a starting point for teachers to plan language arts and English lessons around books that deal with the topic of residential schools. These books have been vetted by various sources and are level appropriate. For example, most of them are listed at GoodMinds, an Indigenous-owned bookstore in Oshweken, Ontario, where a team of educators and cultural resource people evaluate these resources for authenticity, accuracy, and grade level. The literacy connections for each book focus on a particular curricular strand that can be further explored.

Table 1.2. Literacy Curriculum Connections and Resources

CURRICULUM CONNECTIONS	SUGGESTED BOOKS BY GRADE
Primary (K to 3)	
K – Oral Communication – After listening to the story *When We Were Alone*, students may create a collage of their families. Encourage students to discuss the similarities between themselves and the characters from the story. **1 – Reading** – While reading *Nanabosho and the Butterflies*, ask students to identify unfamiliar words. As a group, solve the meaning of these words and connect them to the importance of the story. **2 – Writing** – Read *When I Was Eight*. Use a graphic organizer with students to organize the main ideas in the story. Have students write questions they have regarding these main ideas. **3 – Media Literacy** – After reading *Not My Girl*, ask students to interview each other about the story. As a final task, have students record these interviews with available technology.	**K** – *When We Were Alone* by David Alexander Robertson (2016) **1** – *Nanabosho and the Butterflies* by Joe and Matrine McLellan (2011) **2** – *When I Was Eight* by Christy Jordan-Fenton and Margaret Pokiak-Fenton (2013) **3** – *Not My Girl* by Christy Jordan-Fenton and Margaret Pokiak-Fenton (2014)
Junior (4 to 6)	
4 – Oral Communication – While reading *Kookum's Red Shoes*, ask students to listen "between the lines" to the underlying messages. Have them share these messages. **5 – Reading** – Read *As Long as the Rivers Flow* and ask students to think about the literary devices used in the story. Extend this by having students relay how these devices offered greater insight into the character. **6 – Writing** – After reading *Fatty Legs*, ask students to write a book review of this story. Encourage them to use vivid language to create a tone of importance/necessity in reading about residential schools. **4 to 6 – Media Literacy** – Identify a variety of media texts (e.g., pamphlets, newsletters, blogs) that can be used to discuss the issues in the stories. Analyze the purposes and effects of each media text on the issues.	**4** – *Kookum's Red Shoes* by Peter Eyvindson (2011) **5** – *As Long as the Rivers Flow: A Last Summer Before Residential School* by Constance Brissenden and Larry Oskiniko Loyie (2005) **6** – *Fatty Legs: A True Story* by Christy Jordan-Fenton and Margaret Pokiak-Fenton (2010)
Intermediate (7 and 8)	
7 – Oral Communication – Before reading *My Name Is Seepeetza*, set a listening goal with the class (e.g., listen to create personal connections with the character). Share these insights after the story has been read. **8 – Reading** – While reading *Goodbye Buffalo Bay*, have students think about whose point of view is being represented and whose point of view is missing. Discuss how the other points of view may (or may not) enhance the story.	**7** – *My Name Is Seepeetza* by Shirley Sterling (2004) **8** – *Goodbye Buffalo Bay* by Constance Brissenden and Larry Oskiniko Loyie (2008)

CURRICULUM CONNECTIONS	SUGGESTED BOOKS BY GRADE
7 and 8 – Writing – Gather information on residential schools, and use a graphic organizer to arrange key ideas and dates. Compare this information to the ideas in the stories. **7 and 8 – Media Literacy** – Find several media texts (e.g., newspaper, magazine, blog, podcast, website) that address a key theme or themes from the stories. Analyze the effects of these media texts on the themes.	
Secondary (9 to 12)	
9 – Oral Communication – While reading *Sugar Falls,* have students reflect on the images being produced by the text. Discuss these images in a large group. **10 – Reading and Literature Studies** – Read *Ends/Begins* and have students comment on how the content in the story raises questions about power, values, and culture. **11 – Writing** – Read the *Secret Path.* Have students write a response to the issues raised in this text by including a variety of forms (responses from classmates, research, images, statistics, poetry, other). **12 – Media Studies** – Read *God and the Indian.* Have students identify a variety of media texts that could advertise the key messages in this play. Compare the potential effectiveness (or lack thereof) of these media texts.	**9** – *Sugar Falls: A Residential School Story* by David Alexander Robertson (2011) **10** – *Ends/Begins* by David Alexander Robertson (2010) **11** – *Secret Path* by Gord Downie (2016) **12** – *God and the Indian: A Play* by Drew Hayden Taylor (2014)

The curriculum connections in this table come from modified versions of specific expectations in the Ontario curriculum (elementary language arts and secondary English courses). These strands encourage students to engage with a particular book in a variety of ways.

Indigenous peoples come from oral societies where listening, observing, and speaking were fundamental to transmitting history, values, and worldview (Dion 2014; Toulouse 2016a). Sharing our stories is what helped cultivate our minds and promote creativity. The storyteller drew upon many techniques to illustrate his or her account (e.g., body language, tone of voice, descriptive words and phrases, pauses, embellishment of content). The listener had an equally critical role in observing the storyteller and experiencing these retellings with all the senses (hearing, seeing, tasting, smelling, feeling). A literacy approach that honours these immemorial practices will include engaging narratives written about residential schools.

The books in Table 1.2 provide a safe space for teachers to enter into the conversation about residential schools and their effects on Indigenous peoples. The books also give educators immediate resources for exploring residential-school history with their students. These language arts and English lessons are necessary for developing relations between communities and planning reconciliation activities.

RECONCILIATION ACTIVITIES

Project of Heart (**http://projectofheart.ca/**) is a residential-school healing project that was started by a teacher in Saskatchewan and has spread across the country. It is one of the best examples of how reconciliation can happen as a student-driven and participant-based initiative. It truly embraces the key theme of reconciliation, which is "about establishing and maintaining a mutually respectful relationship between Aboriginal and non-Aboriginal peoples" (TRC 2015, 6). To date, approximately 455 schools and organizations have drawn upon the resources at Project of Heart and completed an activity (or series of activities) focused on reconciliation. The breakdown by province and territory follows below (based upon available data at their website):

- British Columbia – 129
- Alberta – 38
- Saskatchewan – 43
- Manitoba – 69
- Ontario – 135
- Québec – 18
- Nova Scotia – 10
- New Brunswick – 2
- Prince Edward Island – 2
- Newfoundland and Labrador – 8
- Nunavut – 1
- Northwest Territories – no data
- Yukon – no data

The quantitative effects of Project of Heart are staggering, but it is the qualitative effects that stand out for me. I have had the very fortunate experience of hearing from youth and teachers who have been involved in events inspired by Project of Heart. At the 2013 Canadian Teachers' Federation President's Forum in Ottawa, Ontario, a local group of intermediate and secondary students talked about how the stories of residential-school survivors launched them into social action. Students (with the support of their teachers) wrote letters to the prime minister, marched on Parliament Hill, and participated in several human rights tribunals.

I have also witnessed the power of the Kairos Blanket Exercise as a catalyst for change (see figure 1.5, next page). This experiential and hands-on activity tells the colonial story of Indigenous peoples in Canada through a series of fact cards and participant involvement. Blankets are used to represent the country of Canada so that, as each historical and colonial fact is read, the land shrinks for Indigenous peoples. The gift of this exercise is that it concludes with the spirit of hope and provides a space for the participants to discuss what comes next. I have witnessed school administrators committing to policy and curricular change about Indigenous knowledge and Indigenous community connections because of this exercise. I have also witnessed average citizens, so moved by this exercise, publicly recommitting to their own families.

Figure 1.5. Mass Kairos Blanket Exercise on Parliament Hill, June 2016

This activity marked the one-year anniversary of the Truth and Reconciliation Commission of Canada's Calls to Action.

CONCLUSION

I began this chapter with a personal account of my grandmother's experience in residential school. I wish to end it by doing the same. By honouring her story, my story comes to life, as well. My grandmother participated in several residential-school healing activities in our area. However, she felt that so much of the information about residential schools focused on the negative and pointed the finger at the survivors, especially when it came to discussing intergenerational effects and the lack of parenting skills in our communities. She travelled to these events and workshops to learn and reconnect with others, and when she came back home to Sagamok, she was hopeful and dismayed all at once. She often said, "We did the best we could with what we knew" (M. Toulouse, personal communication, April 15, 2011). For me, my grandmother was a living example of someone who endured so much adversity (including genocide) and yet could still have a strong faith and belief in God.

Toward the end of her life, I learned so much about my grandmother. For example, I never knew that she had an Anishinaabe name, Aanakwad Ishpiming. Translated into English, it means "the highest cloud" (ibid.). I think about that name and how it suited her perfectly. She was the matriarch in our family and knew everything that went on with all of us. She could always be counted on for her stories, combined with lots of laughter, lots of good tea, and many lessons to live by.

Chapter 2. Indigenous Peoples of Canada

INTRODUCTION

I went to elementary school in a town that was 10 minutes away from my First Nation. My high school was a 30-minute bus ride on a clear day. When I think about my grade 2 to grade 12 education in the public system, I can definitely say that there were some amazing times and some not-so-good ones, too. That is probably the experience of most Canadians, but what makes my situation a bit different is the long-term effect of the curriculum and content. I never learned much about Indigenous peoples, and what I did learn was highly dismissive and one-dimensional. The lessons very rarely corresponded with what I already knew about my First Nation and did nothing to encourage relationships between me and my non-Indigenous counterparts.

Much has changed since the last time I was a student in secondary school (30 years ago), and I am thankful for the progress we have made. Although our Canadian schools still face challenges with Indigenous education, a movement of transformation has been growing. Some call it the "Seven Fires Prophecies," which I believe to be true. The prophecies speak of a time when Indigenous peoples (especially the youth) lead the way. I can see this today in our school systems, where our people, with our allies, work toward inclusion and fairness. I feel so much pride when I witness our children (Indigenous and non-Indigenous) coming together in educational spaces that honour First Nation, Métis, and Inuit knowledge, values, and traditions.

Incorporating the worldviews and contributions of Indigenous peoples is now the policy of most school boards across Canada. The final report of the Truth and Reconciliation Commission of Canada (TRC) reaffirmed this priority. The Call to Action "implementing Kindergarten to Grade Twelve curriculum … on Aboriginal peoples in Canadian history" (TRC 2015, 331) is necessary for healing between nations to occur.

WHAT ARE THE SEVEN FIRES PROPHECIES?

The Seven Fires Prophecies come from the teachings of the Anishinaabek and predate the arrival of Europeans. These prophecies, or fires, each foretold a future era in the life of the people on Turtle Island (North America). At the time of the seventh fire — believed to be happening today — a new generation would emerge as leaders who would work to join all nations on Turtle Island. This stage is crucial for human and other-than-human existence, and represents a monumental shift in the way all human beings behave on Mother Earth.

Once again, this Call to Action is why this chapter on First Nation, Métis, and Inuit peoples is included. It is an introduction, with curriculum ideas and identified resources for educators to use in elementary and secondary classrooms. It provides links to trustworthy websites, informative statistics, and key content to help make this Call to Action come to life in K to 12 classrooms.

We begin with some basic facts to inform our conversation:

- The Constitution of Canada recognizes three distinct groups of Indigenous peoples: First Nations, Métis, and Inuit. Section 35 of the Constitution also recognizes and affirms Indigenous rights (TRC 2015).

- There are 60 distinct Indigenous languages in Canada, belonging to 12 language families. Each Indigenous language can also have several dialects. For example, the Cree language has eight dialects in which words or phrases can be very different (Statistics Canada 2017a).

- Indigenous peoples in Canada are associated with six unique geo-cultural areas. These areas are the Arctic, Eastern Woodlands (also known as Northeast), Northwest Coast, Plains, Plateau, and the Subarctic (Canadian Museum of History 2017). (See figure 2.1.)

Figure 2.1. Geo-cultural Areas of Canada's Indigenous Peoples

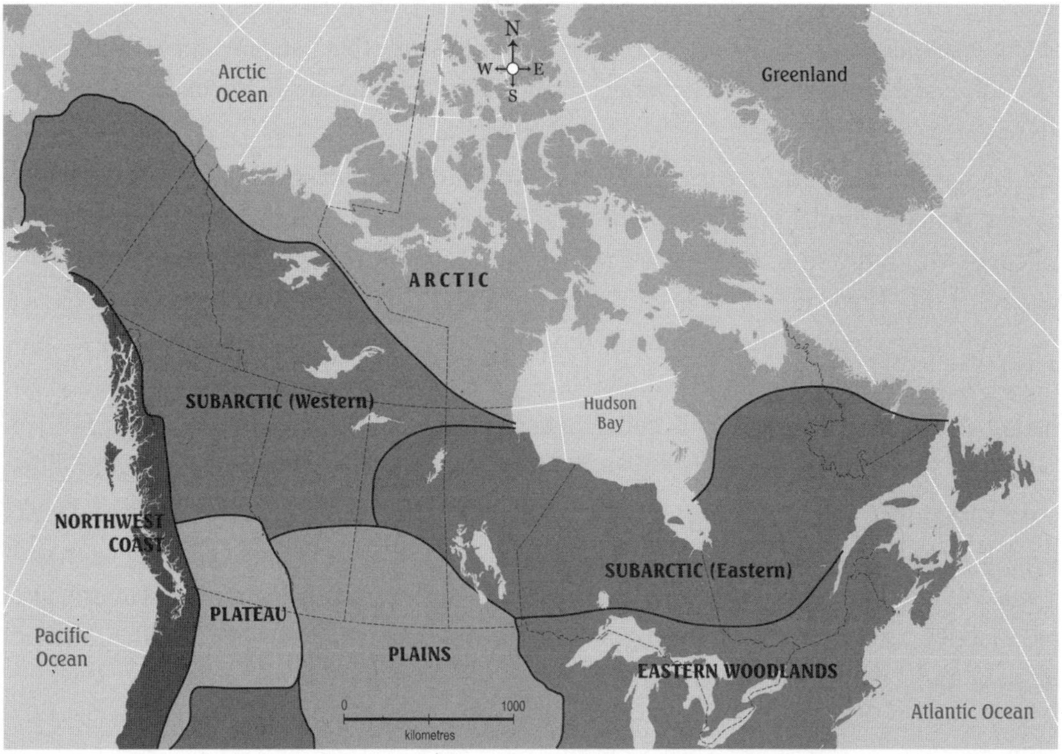

- A total of 1.4 million people identifies as Indigenous, which represents four percent of Canada's population (Statistics Canada 2017b). (See table 2.1.)

Table 2.1. Population of Indigenous Peoples in Canada by Province and Territory

PROVINCE/TERRITORY	POPULATION IDENTIFYING AS INDIGENOUS*	
Newfoundland and Labrador	35 795* First Nations: 19 315	Métis: 7660 Inuk (Inuit): 6265
Prince Edward Island	2230* First Nations: 1520	Métis: 410 Inuk (Inuit): 55
Nova Scotia	33 850* First Nations: 21 895	Métis: 10 050 Inuk (Inuit): 700
New Brunswick	22 620* First Nations: 16 115	Métis: 4850 Inuk (Inuit): 485
Québec	141 910* First Nations: 82 420	Métis: 40 960 Inuk (Inuit): 12 575
Ontario	301 430* First Nations: 201 100	Métis: 86 015 Inuk (Inuit): 3360
Manitoba	195 900* First Nations: 114 225	Métis: 78 835 Inuk (Inuit): 580
Saskatchewan	157 740* First Nations: 103 205	Métis: 52 450 Inuk (Inuit): 295
Alberta	220 695* First Nations: 116 670	Métis: 96 870 Inuk (Inuit): 1990
British Columbia	232 290* First Nations: 155 015	Métis: 69 470 Inuk (Inuit): 1570
Yukon	7710* First Nations: 6585	Métis: 845 Inuk (Inuit): 175
Northwest Territories	21 160* First Nations: 13 350	Métis: 3245 Inuk (Inuit): 4335
Nunavut	27 365* First Nations: 125	Métis: 130 Inuk (Inuit): 27 070

* Totals are not complete because some people list multiple identities and/or Indigenous identity not included elsewhere.

This data comes from Statistics Canada's National Household Survey of 2011. It is the most recent information on Indigenous populations in Canada.

TRADITIONAL VALUES VS. TECHNOLOGICAL VALUES

Indigenous nations in Canada have richly diverse cultures, languages, traditions, and ceremonies. However, they have traditional values that were (and are) shared among all (Indigenous Corporate Training Inc. 2017). One such value is mutual respect between Indigenous peoples and the Earth and all its occupants, including stones and rivers, which are regarded as living. Another value is that of stewardship and taking care of the land, rooted in immemorial understanding of human environmental impact. However, many of these traditional values have been diminished by colonization, consumerism, and technological dependence (Indigenous Works 2017). They have survived through the cultural practices of ancestral stories and teachings told or kept by Elders and knowledge keepers.

Although many of these practices were forced to go underground, they have stood the test of time. For example, in the Haudenosaunee community, the two-row wampum belt is a reminder of the teachings that Indigenous and non-Indigenous cultures can only live in peace if each nation respects the other's way of life (see figure 2.2.). Conflict is resolved only through coming together to discuss solutions in a meaningful way.

Figure 2.2. Onondaga Elder Oren Lyons and a Replica of the Two-Row Wampum Belt

This photo documents a historic renewal campaign in 2013 that commemorated the 400th anniversary of an agreement made between the Haudenosaunee and the Dutch government in 1613. The commemoration was held to raise awareness about the two-row wampum belt and its importance for the next seven generations.

Traditional Indigenous values and technological values – those mainstream beliefs and practices that shape our modern world – are systemically at odds (ibid.). Indigenous youth face the biggest struggles, because they are immersed both in a technological world with one set of principles and a traditional one that has an entirely different worldview (Indigenous Corporate Training Inc. 2017). Table 2.2 compares these values, highlighting their potential conflicts.

Truth and Reconciliation in Canadian Schools

Table 2.2. Traditional Indigenous Values and Technological Society Values

TRADITIONAL VALUE	TECHNOLOGICAL VALUE
Aging is a natural and welcomed process.	Youth and staying young are paramount.
Humour is a sign of trust.	Humour has its place.
Cooperation between each other is essential.	Competition is a driving force in life.
Eye contact is not necessary for meaningful communication.	Eye contact suggests that you are listening and/or telling the truth.
Silence is important. Gaps in conversation are natural.	Talking is important. Filling the space avoids discomfort.
Feasts often begin by honouring the spirits and ancestors first.	Feasts are formalized into dates and are often secular in nature.
Focus is on community and sharing.	Focus is on individual and property/rights.

These seven values have been selected because they are the most relevant today. Each contrasting value can be vetted through examining our own lives, popular culture, and social media. (Indigenous Works; ICTINC)

THE INDIAN ACT OF 1876

The Indian Act of 1876 is a piece of legislation created for the purposes of subjugating Indigenous peoples (First Nations & Indigenous Studies, UBC 2017). It framed the way that non-Indigenous Canadians would ultimately view and treat the First Peoples of this land. Although it has undergone several amendments, its effects still resonate in negative ways in Indigenous communities today (Joseph 2017). It is a living document with systemic inequity, racism, and sexism built into it.

Among its many provisions, the Indian Act:

- created reserves and then forced Indigenous peoples to get permission from the Indian Agent to leave those reserves
- enforced an unfair permit system on reserves for those who wanted to farm and sell their goods, and regulated the cutting of firewood for home use
- ensured that reserve lands had no value, and that Indigenous peoples could not own the land, only occupy it, and therefore could not receive loans for development
- expropriated reserve lands for the use of non-Indigenous municipalities, businesses, and citizens. In some cases, whole communities were relocated as a result.
- outlawed traditions, ceremonies, and languages, and introduced residential schools
- forced those who wanted to go to university to enfranchise (or give up their status/identity/rights)
- imposed divisive band council election systems and denied communities the right to form political organizations

- registered all those identified as "Indians" and Inuit by assigning European names (often French or British in origin)
- denied Indigenous peoples the right to vote in provincial and federal elections
- took away First Nations status/identity/rights of Indigenous women who married non-Indigenous men, but gave First Nations status/identity/rights to non-Indigenous women who married Indigenous men. This provision displaced entire generations of children and families.

If you notice, reserves are typically located away from towns and cities, often on lands of lower quality. This approach was highly intentional, isolating Indigenous peoples and making them invisible to the public (First Nations & Indigenous Studies, University of British Columbia 2017). Meanwhile governments, corporations, and non-Indigenous Canadians retained the best lands and resources, enabling them to prosper over the last 140-plus years. According to the TRC's final report, the Indian Act and its provisions creating reserves and their third-world conditions were hurting entire generations of First Peoples (TRC 2015).

The negative effects of the Indian Act continue to be loss of language, culture, health, and life, along with lower educational attainment. For example, Indigenous peoples have the highest rates of diabetes, lower graduation rates and participation in STEM fields, and the highest rates of suicide and incarceration. The positive outcomes include the strengths of Indigenous peoples, whose resiliency resulted in newfound hope. For example, the Seven Fires Prophecies predicted that Indigenous youth would one day seek out traditions and lead us, as they are doing today. Spirituality and healing, in both the resurgence of traditional ceremonies and the legitimacy of traditional knowledge (including environmental knowledge) to understand and heal the Earth from climate change, are also sources of hope.

WHAT I KNOW ABOUT FIRST NATIONS

I have had the honour of going to school and working in various First Nation territories across Canada. Diverse, proud, and gifted with humour are the three attributes that always come to mind when I think about First Nation peoples. I am so lucky that I was raised in Sagamok First Nation (on the north shore of Lake Huron, one and a half hours west of Sudbury, Ontario). I believe that each of the six hundred First Nation communities in Canada offers so much richness in its knowledge, values, and traditions (see figure 2.3).

Many First Nation traditions are rooted in the land. Growing up in Sagamok, I remember my favourite celebrations by the seasons. The spring evokes my best memories of the sugar bush at our family farm when I was a child. Known as *Ziisbaakdoke Giizis* (Sugar Moon) in Ojibwe, this season had so many teachings that went with it. It was not only about collecting sap to make maple syrup and maple taffy; it was about our family being together, working together, and learning together. It was here that I was immersed in the teachings of patience, as well as love and respect for nature.

Truth and Reconciliation in Canadian Schools

As an adult, the fall meant that *Tasehwung* (Feasting for Ancestors) was close. This tradition has become the most significant one for me now. In late October and early November, we honour our dead through feasting and sacred fires. We clean the graves of our families and put out wreaths with long ribbons for them. The wreaths are made from red willow, cedar, and a variety of pine boughs. Ribbons meant to represent colours that were of importance to the individual are added. We believe that our ancestors use these wreaths to travel the land during this season. The wreath is a symbol of our ancestors' ability to travel in spirit throughout the Earth.

Figure 2.3. First Nations in Canada

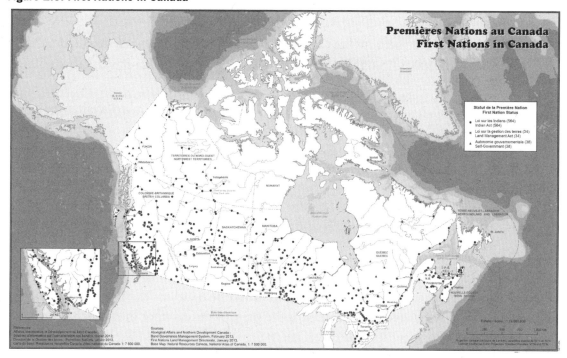

An interactive version of this map can be seen at <http://fnpim-cippn.aandc-aadnc.gc.ca/index-eng.html>.

We begin our feast by preparing a spirit plate (bits of food from all items at the feast) to be offered to the sacred fire. Each family member is given tobacco (a sacred medicine) to put in the fire as they offer the names of the ancestors they wish to remember. After all have had their say, the spirit plate is offered in prayer. It is said that the spirits (our ancestors) eat first in this offering, and then we honour them by feasting.

The information below is from Statistics Canada (2017c). However, I encourage educators to connect with First Nation communities to gain a broader (and more personal) picture.

- First Nation peoples represent 2.6 percent of the total Canadian population
- almost one-quarter of First Nation peoples live in Ontario, while most others live in the western provinces and the territories
- 49.3 percent of registered Indians (i.e., First Nation peoples who are registered under the Indian Act and often referred to as status Indians) live on a reserve
- 25.1 percent of First Nation peoples are defined as "not registered Indians," with the majority living in the Atlantic provinces

- 44.8 percent of First Nation peoples aged 25 to 64 have some type of post-secondary qualification (university degree – 8.7 percent; university certificate – 3.6 percent; college diploma – 19.4 percent, trades certificate – 13.2 percent)
- 60.2 percent of First Nation peoples aged 25 to 64 have a high-school diploma
- off-reserve First Nation peoples have higher graduation rates than on-reserve First Nation peoples for both secondary and post-secondary levels

The following organizations offer a wealth of information about First Nation peoples:

- Assembly of First Nations, **http://www.afn.ca/home/** – The national voice for First Nation peoples in Canada
- Indigenous and Northern Affairs Canada, First Nations, **https://www.aadnc-aandc. gc.ca/eng/1100100013791/1100100013795** – Federal government representative of First Nations in Canada
- Native Women's Association of Canada, **http://www.nwac.ca/** – Umbrella organization for 13 First Nation, Métis, and Inuit women's organizations in Canada
- National Association of Friendship Centres, **http://nafc.ca/en/** – A network of friendship centres from coast to coast that serve off-reserve First Nation, Métis, and Inuit peoples

WHAT I KNOW ABOUT THE INUIT

In 2013, I had the privilege of hearing Inuit leader Mary Simon (now special representative on Arctic issues for the Minister of Indigenous and Northern Affairs) talk about the importance of cultural identity and education for Inuit youth. I was captivated by her clear message that the land and the people are interconnected and that the gaps in education for Inuit youth need to be reconciled. Her keynote at the Canadian Teachers' Federation Forum on First Nations, Métis, and Inuit education inspired me to learn more about her nation.

According to Statistics Canada (ibid.), 73.1 percent of Inuit peoples live in their traditional territories of Inuit Nunangat, with the largest number living in Nunavut (see figure 2.4). Of the remaining 26.9 percent who live outside their territory, approximately 4 out of 10 live in urban centres (e.g., Edmonton, Montreal, Ottawa-Gatineau, Yellowknife, St. John's). The Inuktitut language is spoken by 83 percent of people living in Inuit Nunangat (Statistics Canada 2017a) and has several dialects that vary by region. The challenges facing the Inuit peoples range from climate change and housing to educational attainment.

Following are some basic facts:

- The Inuit represent slightly less than 1 percent of the total Canadian population.
- Just over one-third (35.6 percent) of Inuit aged 25 to 64 have some type of post-secondary qualification (university degree – 5.1 percent; university certificate – 1.7 percent; college diploma – 15.6 percent; trades certificate – 13.2 percent).
- Inuit who live outside their traditional territories have a higher rate of post-secondary education than those living in traditional territories.
- Two-fifths (41 percent) of Inuit aged 25 to 64 have a high-school diploma.

I highly recommend the following organizations as a starting point for learning from the Inuit themselves:

- Inuit Tapiriit Kanatami, **https://www.itk.ca/** – national voice of Canada's 60 000 Inuit
- Inuit Broadcasting Corporation, **http://www.inuitbroadcasting.ca/** – award-winning television programming for Inuit
- Inuit Women of Canada, **http://pauktuutit.ca/** – national organization of Inuit women
- Inuit Art Foundation, **http://www.inuitartfoundation.org/#** – non-profit organization supporting Inuit work
- Inuit Circumpolar Council Canada, **http://www.inuitcircumpolar.com/** – international voice on protecting Inuit way of life

Figure 2.4. Inuit Communities in Canada

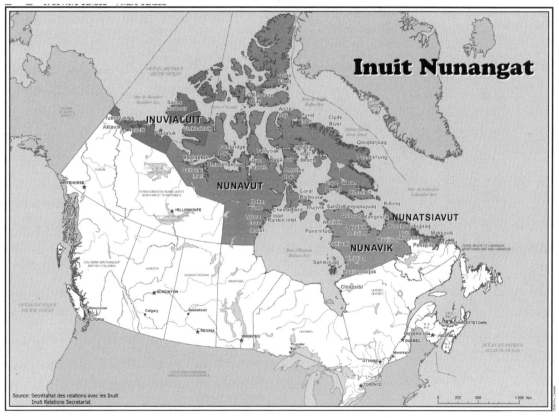

An interactive version of this map can be found at <www.aadnc-aandc.gc.ca/Map/irs/mp/index-en.html>.

WHAT I KNOW ABOUT THE MÉTIS

On April 14, 2016, history was made when Métis people and non-status Indigenous peoples were ruled to be "Indians" by the Supreme Court of Canada (see figure 2.5). This ruling meant that Métis and non-status peoples, at long last, could hold the federal government accountable for their rights and treaty claims (as already established with First Nation and Inuit peoples).

I have had the honour of knowing Métis people all my life. My father, Nelson Toulouse, has a long-standing friendship with Tony Belcourt, the founding president of the Métis Nation of Ontario, and my husband, Luc Watier, is also Métis. What always stands out for me about the Métis is their deep sense of kinship, history, and dedication to change. One of my own role models is Senator Thelma Villeneuve Chalifoux, who was the first Métis woman to be appointed to the Senate (among many other firsts). She raised seven children on her own and represents the strength that our Indigenous women possess. I am fortunate to have these personal connections to the Métis Nation in my private life and professional world.

Figure 2.5. Gabriel Daniels After Supreme Court Ruling on Métis Rights

Gabriel Daniels won constitutional recognition of the rights of Métis and non-status Indians under the Constitution of Canada, completing the legal challenge launched 17 years earlier by his father, Harry Daniels, then-leader of the Congress of Aboriginal Peoples.

The following information is from Statistics Canada (2017a; 2017b; 2017c):

- Métis people represent 30 percent of the total Indigenous population.
- Only 2.4 percent of Métis speak an Indigenous language, with Cree and Denesuline being the most common; however, 810 individuals speak the traditional Michif language.
- Métis have the highest French-English bilingualism rate among Indigenous peoples.
- 55 percent of Métis aged 25 to 64 have completed some type of post-secondary education.
- 20 percent of Métis aged 25 to 64 do not have a secondary diploma, with the largest number in the Atlantic provinces of Prince Edward Island, Newfoundland and Labrador, and New Brunswick.

Truth and Reconciliation in Canadian Schools

I encourage educators to connect with Métis communities to gain a broader and more personal picture and to establish relationships. I also recommend exploring the following links as a start to this process:

- Métis National Council, **http://www.metisnation.ca/** – national organization that represents Métis people
- Métis Nation of Ontario, **http://www.metisnation.org** – comprehensive website with cultural and language resources
- Manitoba Métis Federation, **http://www.mmf.mb.ca/index.php** – wide-ranging historical and youth information
- Virtual Museum of Métis History and Culture, **http://www.metismuseum.ca/index.php** – world's largest and richest collection of primary sources
- Métis Nation BC Education, **http://www.mnbc.ca/documents-resources/education** – cross-curricular units on Métis

WHY THE ARTS ARE AN IDEAL APPROACH TO TEACHING ABOUT THE INDIGENOUS PEOPLES OF CANADA

Drama, dance, music, and visual arts are creative, emotionally moving, interrelated disciplines that nurture the whole student (physical, emotional, intellectual, spiritual). These practices are consistent with one of the many ways that Indigenous peoples learn and connect with classroom content (Smith-Gilman 2015; Toulouse 2016b). Accordingly, I have chosen an arts-based pedagogy to engage all K to 12 learners in exploring their understanding about Indigenous peoples of Canada. Table 2.3 includes grade-appropriate Indigenous books that relate to specific aspects of the arts in each division (primary, junior, intermediate, and secondary).

Table 2.3. The Arts Curriculum Connections and Resources

CURRICULUM CONNECTIONS	SUGGESTED BOOKS BY GRADE
Primary (K to 3)	
K – Dance – While reading *Powwow Counting in Cree*, encourage students to communicate their understanding of the numbers in the book through movement (e.g., show the number 4 in a variety of ways – hands, bodies, materials). **1 – Drama** – After reading *Giving Thanks: A Native American Good Morning Message,* guide students in forming tableaus that reflect key scenes in the story. **2 – Music** – Read *Owls See Clearly at Night: A Michif Alphabet.* Re-read using a simple and familiar rhythm (e.g., ABC). Discuss the difference that music makes in the retelling. **3 – Visual Arts** – While reading *SkySisters,* ask students to describe the techniques of the illustrator (e.g., use of colour, lines, texture). Discuss the effectiveness of these techniques.	**K** – *Powwow Counting in Cree* by Penny M. Thomas (2013) **1** – *Giving Thanks: A Native American Good Morning Message* by Jake Swamp (2002) **2** – *Owls See Clearly at Night: A Michif Alphabet* by Julie Flett (2010) **3** – *SkySisters* by Jan Bourdeau Waboose (2000)

CURRICULUM CONNECTIONS	SUGGESTED BOOKS BY GRADE

Junior (4 to 6)

4 – Dance – While reading *A Walk on the Tundra,* ask students to translate these nature scenes into movement (e.g., how do these flowers, mosses, shrubs, and lichens move in the story?).	**4** – *A Walk on the Tundra* by Anna Ziegler and Rebecca Hainnu (2011)
5 – Drama – Read *The Secret of Your Name,* and ask students how the mood of the story could be enhanced at certain points (e.g., dimming lights, using music).	**5** – *The Secret of Your Name* by David Bouchard (2009)
6 – Music – After reading *Raven Brings the Light,* ask students to identify a style of music that would complement a public reading of this book (e.g., jazz, pop, rap, drum, classical).	**6** – *Raven Brings the Light* by Roy Henry Vickers and Robert Budd (2013)
4 to 6 – Visual Arts – Use mixed media (e.g., photographs, images, transfers, photocopies) to create a personal response to the book students have read.	

Intermediate (7 and 8)

7 – Dance – While reading *The Night Wanderer: A Graphic Novel,* use an element of dance (supported by music) to convey moods in the story (e.g., recurring sequence of movement with sounds for scary scenes).	**7** – *The Night Wanderer: A Graphic Novel* by Drew Hayden Taylor (2013)
8 – Drama – After reading *The Shaman's Nephew: A Life in the Far North,* have students create a one-minute soundscape (with movement) to accompany the beginning and the ending of the story.	**8** – *The Shaman's Nephew: A Life in the Far North* by Simon Tookoome and Sheldon Oberman (2000)
7 and 8 – Music – Create a musical composition for the book students have read by using instruments or found sounds/recycled materials. Ask students to explain how the composition connects to the story.	
7 and 8 – Visual Arts – Construct a new book cover for the book students have read using the techniques of the collograph (relief printing using cardboard with attached shapes and fibres).	

Secondary (9 to 12)

9 – Dance – While reading *The Lynching of Louie Sam,* have students select five gestures described in the story. Ask them to create a sixteen-bar movement phrase with these gestures.	**9** – *The Lynching of Louie Sam* by Elizabeth Stewart (2012)
10 – Drama – While reading *Betty: The Helen Betty Osborne Story,* have students use voice/movement techniques to support atmosphere in the story (e.g., mimic the rain and feelings of despair).	**10** – *Betty: The Helen Betty Osborne Story* by David Alexander Robertson (2015)

Truth and Reconciliation in Canadian Schools

CURRICULUM CONNECTIONS	SUGGESTED BOOKS BY GRADE
11 – Music – Read *The 500 Years of Resistance Comic Book.* Use GarageBand to create a soundtrack that represents the story. Ask them to describe how their track connects to this book. **12 – Visual Arts** – Read *The Inconvenient Indian: A Curious Account of Native People in North America.* Have students produce art works that communicate various points of view in this book (e.g., Indians and cowboys in film/pop culture). Extend this by having students examine how these points of view affected society's perceptions of Indigenous peoples.	**11** – *The 500 Years of Resistance Comic Book* by Gord Hill (2010) **12** – *The Inconvenient Indian: A Curious Account of Native People in North America* by Thomas King (2012)

The curriculum connections in this table come from modified versions of specific expectations in the Ontario curriculum (elementary and secondary arts courses). These subjects engage students with a particular book in a variety of ways.

CONCLUSION

June 21 of every year marks National Indigenous Peoples Day in Canada, when hundreds of events are held across the country. While I am a keen advocate for the integration of Indigenous knowledge and culture across the school curriculum, I believe it is vital for all schools to participate in targeted relationship-building activities. I view National Indigenous Peoples Day as the ideal culminating task for students in celebrating the Indigenous peoples of Canada. To find events that are near you (or to plan an event), go to the Indigenous and Northern Affairs Canada website: https://www.aadnc-aandc.gc.ca/eng/1100100013331/1100100013332.

Chapter 3. Treaties of Canada

Call 62.i. – Education for Reconciliation (TRC Calls to Action)

"We call upon the federal, provincial, and territorial governments, in consultation and collaboration with Survivors, Aboriginal peoples, and educators, to make age-appropriate curriculum on …Treaties … a mandatory education requirement for Kindergarten to Grade 12 students."

INTRODUCTION

Every July in my home community of Sagamok First Nation, we have a large celebration called "Treaty Day." This day is dedicated to the Robinson-Huron Treaty of 1850, which my First Nation signed. Community members young and old gather to visit a variety of information booths (e.g., services in the area), share stories, and feast together. Part of this day is the issuing of treaty payments to each member by a representative of the federal government (typically from Indigenous and Northern Affairs Canada). We line up and show our Indian status cards, and the agent checks our name off the federal list of registered Indians. The agent then gives us $4.00 each as descendants of the original signatories to this pre-Confederation treaty – the equivalent amount to the payment in 1850, which was a bag of flour and a bag of potatoes. The $4.00 payment, in my view, is a major problem. These treaty payments have not increased in 167 years.

In its Calls to Action, the 2015 Truth and Reconciliation Commission of Canada (TRC) states that "age-appropriate curriculum on …Treaties … [become] a mandatory education requirement for Kindergarten to Grade 12 students" (TRC, 331). I completely agree. The curriculum has to be authentic and honest. It also has to elaborate on the fact that the treaty rights of Indigenous peoples have been widely ignored. My own nation's treaty (Robinson-Huron) was negotiated in good faith by my ancestors. So how is it that for 167 years it has still not been honoured by the Crown (now the Government of Canada)? Why is it that our communities continue to be the poorest in the land?

The Crown inserted an escalation clause in the Robinson-Huron Treaty (and other treaties in Canada) to try and cap the annuities to be paid to Indigenous peoples. This escalation clause was an attempt by several representatives of the Crown to take the lands of Indigenous peoples for no future increased costs. Several records and affidavits confirm that the original Ojibwe signatories to the various Robinson Treaties did not agree with this clause. The Robinson-Huron Treaty had a provision in it that said "…or such further sum as Her Majesty may be graciously pleased to order" about increasing the annuities, based upon resource extraction profits in mining and such (Robinson-Huron Treaty 1850). This statement is the basis for current claims that these increased annuities are 167 years overdue and should be paid. A court case on this issue has been initiated.

K to 12 treaty education requires a truthful approach that compares the intent of those treaties with the realities. This approach offers the facts and provides insight into who has really benefitted from these legal contracts. We begin here with some of those facts.

- There are 70 historic treaties in Canada (1701 to 1923) that cover 50 percent of the country's land mass (see figure 3.1). The rest of Canada is covered by peace and/or friendship treaties, modern treaties, and comprehensive land claims (Indigenous and Northern Affairs Canada 2017; Land Claims Agreements Coalition 2017).

- Treaties are legally binding agreements between nations. The term *Nation to Nation* applies when discussing treaties with Indigenous peoples in Canada today (Historica Canada 2017).

- Treaties and the inherent rights of Indigenous peoples are guaranteed under Section 35 of the Constitution of Canada. This Constitution governs all Canadians.

- Indigenous peoples view treaties as sacred and have honoured their end of these agreements. Most non-Indigenous governments have not honoured the treaties they signed with Indigenous peoples in North America (Early Canadiana Online 2017).

Figure 3.1. Treaties in Canada

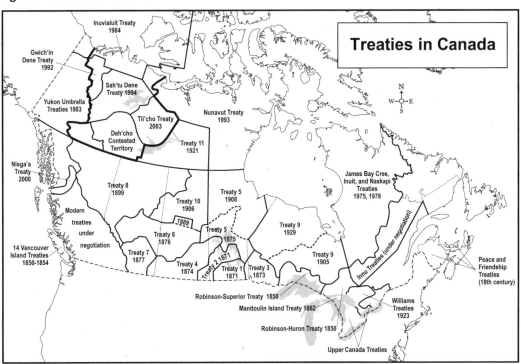

Nearly the entire landmass of Canada is treaty territory or current land-claims territory. All Canadian citizens therefore live on the traditional lands of Indigenous peoples.

DIFFERING VIEWS ON TREATIES

There are two differing views on treaties: (1) the Crown or government perspective, and (2) the Indigenous perspective. When the treaties were signed, representatives from both groups were present. The Crown brought their paper and pens, laws, and colonial worldview. The Indigenous peoples brought their traditions, values, and intimate connections with the land. The Crown "saw treaties as a way to legalize the ceding of Indian lands to clear the way for European settlement" (Goldi Productions Ltd. 2017, 1). Indigenous peoples saw "treaties [as] solemn pacts establishing the future basis of relations between [nations]" (ibid.). At no time did Indigenous peoples see treaties as giving up their lands or consenting to be assimilated. The conflict in values between both groups is even more apparent today. Some of the long-lasting differences include the following:

- Land was, and is, viewed as both communal and sacred by Indigenous peoples. Land was, and is, viewed as property by the government (Office of the Treaty Commissioner 2017).

- Wampum belts and oral history were, and are, viewed as revered agreements by Indigenous peoples. Treaties (signed papers) were, and are, viewed by government as secular and subject to future change.

- Payment for signing treaties was seen as a gift and a respectful gesture from settler governments to Indigenous peoples. Such payment was seen by governments as Indigenous peoples selling their lands (Early Canadiana Online 2017).

These divergent views continue to be prominent in treaty interpretations and negotiations today. They have become the foundation – usually unacknowledged – of the discourse surrounding treaties in Canada. This conflict in values explains why it is essential to have K to 12 treaty education in all schools.

SUMMARY OF SELECT TREATIES AND RELEVANT ACTS

Peace and Friendship Treaties: The first peace and friendship treaty was signed by the Mi'kmaq, Maliseet, and Passamaquoddy with the British in 1725. It covered the northeastern United States, Nova Scotia, and New Brunswick. The intent of such treaties was to ensure that Indigenous peoples and settlers in those territories could live side by side.

Royal Proclamation of 1763: Signed between Indigenous nations and the British, the intent of this proclamation was to ensure that future agreements were made publicly in the form of treaties. The proclamation clarified that Indigenous peoples would continue to exercise their right to hunt and fish in territories occupied by settlers.

Pre-Confederation Treaties:

- **The Niagara Treaty of 1764**

    This treaty was signed between the British and 24 Indigenous nations. The intent was to reaffirm the relationship between nations and to guarantee that annual gifts would be given to Indigenous peoples.

- **The Treaty of Paris (1783)**

  This treaty created the United States and Canadian border. It ignored earlier agreements and promises made to Indigenous peoples. It is important because it resulted in two tracts of land being transferred to the Haudenosaunee, land now known as *Oshweken* (Six Nations).

- **The Jay Treaty of 1794**

  This treaty, signed between Britain and the United States, specified that Indigenous peoples could cross the border freely between the two countries.

- **The Selkirk Treaty of 1817**

  Negotiated between British aristocrat Thomas Selkirk and the Hudson's Bay Company, the Selkirk Treaty covered lands in southern Manitoba and eventually became the Red River Settlement. It was highly controversial because it ignored the Métis peoples of that area and their traditional land use. This land changed hands many times, which led to the Red River Resistance of 1870.

- **The Bond Head Treaties of 1836**

  These treaties were written to move Indigenous peoples in Ontario to Manitoulin Island and other islands in Lake Huron to keep them separate from settlers.

- **The Robinson Treaties of 1850**

  These treaties set aside a significant portion of land in northern Ontario for Indigenous peoples and guaranteed the continuation of their hunting and fishing rights in these territories. They also specified annuity payments by the government for settler use of traditional lands.

- **The Douglas Treaties (1850–54)**

  These treaties set aside farming lands on Vancouver Island for Indigenous peoples and stated that other so-called surrendered lands could be rightfully used for hunting and fishing. These treaties included a gift element whereby Indigenous peoples were presented with payment (e.g., cash, clothing, and blankets).

British North America Act of 1867: Section 91 of this Act stated that the federal government had constitutional responsibility for Indigenous nations in Canada. Treaty-making was also now the responsibility of the Prime Minister.

The Numbered Treaties:

- **Treaties One to Five (1871–75)**

  These treaties guaranteed Indigenous signatories and their descendants lands to live on, treaty payments, monies for blankets, hunting and fishing rights, farming assistance, and schools.

- **Treaty Six (1876) and Treaty Seven (1877)**

  The provisions in these treaties were similar to the first five numbered ones. However, Treaty Six included health care in its terms.

- Treaties Eight to Eleven (1899–1921)

  Although these contained similar provisions to the first five treaties, Treaty Eight was unique in including many small tracts of land for family groupings.

The Williams Treaties: These treaties of 1923 covered much of southern and central Ontario. They had similar provisions to the numbered treaties. However, the right to hunt, fish, and trap on treaty lands (other than reserves) was removed.

Modern Treaties and Land Claims:

- The James Bay and Northern Québec Agreement (1975)

  This agreement was the first modern land-claim agreement in Canada and included $225 million paid to the Inuit and Cree peoples of northern Québec. Under its terms, the Inuit and Cree also ceded portions of their northern traditional territory to allow a hydroelectric dam to be built by the province of Québec.

- The Inuvialuit Claims Settlement Act (1984)

  This act gave the Inuit of the Western Arctic legal control of their natural resources. It was signed to protect the wildlife, lands, and culture of the people.

- The Nunavut Land Claims Agreement (1993)

  This agreement led to the creation of Nunavut in 1999. It specified rights and payment for lands.

- The Nisga'a Treaty (1996)

  This treaty, an example of self-government, covered areas in northwestern British Columbia. Its terms included control of natural resources and payment for lands.

WHAT IS SELF-GOVERNMENT?

Self-government agreements – negotiated with federal and provincial or territorial governments – give Indigenous communities greater control and law-making authority, including social and economic development, education, health, lands, and more. The right to self-government, however, is not guaranteed in the Constitution. Individual Indigenous communities have achieved differing levels of self-government through the land claims (or comprehensive claim settlement) process, not through constitutional amendment. Many of Canada's First Nation communities are still governed by the Indian Act of 1876 and are referred to as "bands." This means that their reserve lands, monies, other resources, and governance structure are managed by the provisions in the Indian Act.

In the United States, Indian tribes are recognized as "domestic, dependent, sovereign nations" with inherent rights to govern within their reserves, to make laws, to establish courts, and to enjoy immunity from external lawsuits. This doctrine of domestic sovereignty has never been applied in Canada (INAC 2017).

- Yukon Final Agreements (1993–2016)

  Of the 14 First Nations in Yukon, 11 have negotiated final agreements with the federal government that give them decision-making powers on their lands, including natural resources and taxation.

- **Constitution Act of 1982:** Section 25 of the Charter of Rights and Freedoms guaranteed the rights and freedoms of all Aboriginal, Métis, and Inuit peoples (with reference to the provisions in the Royal Proclamation of 1763 and all previous and outstanding land claim agreements). Section 35 of this Act recognized and affirmed existing treaty rights.

For more detailed information on treaties by province and territory, see the suggested resources in table 3.1. The websites provide current information about the treaties, lands, and culture of Indigenous peoples in these areas.

Table 3.1. Indigenous Treaty, Land, and Culture Resources by Province and Territory

PROVINCE/ TERRITORY	SUGGESTED RESOURCE WEBSITES
Newfoundland and Labrador	http://www.innu.ca/ Website of the Innu Nation, the governing body for the Labrador Innu. Provides information on Innu communities, their culture and history, Innu rights and government, Innu youth, etc. http://qalipu.ca/ Website of the Qalipu Mi'kmaq First Nation Band, with comprehensive information. Qalipu (pronounced *ha-lee-boo,* meaning "caribou") has no reserve land, but is made up of 66 traditional Mi'kmaq communities. http://www.nunatukavut.ca/home/ Website of the Inuit of NunatuKavut ("our ancient land"), the Southern Inuit, who live mainly in southern and central Labrador.
Prince Edward Island	http://www.ncpei.com/ Website of the Native Council of Prince Edward Island, the self- governing authority for all off-reserve Indigenous people living on Epekwitk (PEI), most of whom are descendants of the original Mi'kmaq people who inhabited the Island. http://www.mcpei.ca/ Website of the Mi'kmaq Confederacy of Prince Edward Island, the united voice for the advancement of treaty and Indigenous rights for Lennox Island and Abegweit First Nations. http://www.apcfnc.ca/ The Atlantic Policy Congress of First Nations Chiefs Secretariat is a policy research and advocacy secretariat for 32 Mi'kmaq, Maliseet, Passamaquoddy, and Innu chiefs, nations, and communities in Atlantic Canada, Québec, and Maine in the United States. Downloadable educational posters on various First Nation treaties.
Nova Scotia	http://www.unsi.ns.ca/ Website of the Union of Nova Scotia Indians, a tribal council created in 1969 to provide a unified political voice for the Mi'kmaq people of Nova Scotia. Information on historic court decisions and current news. http://ncns.ca/ Native Council of Nova Scotia, the self-governing authority for the large community of Mi'kmaq and Indigenous peoples living off-reserve in Nova Scotia throughout traditional Mi'kmaq territory. Wealth of historical information and programs and services offered.

PROVINCE/ TERRITORY	SUGGESTED RESOURCE WEBSITES
Nova Scotia (continued)	http://mikmaqrights.com/negotiations/treaties/ Website of the Mi'kmaq Rights Initiative or *Kwilmu'kw Maw-klusuaqn* ("we are seeking consensus"), the forum for Mi'kmaq peoples, Nova Scotia, and Canada to resolve issues related to Mi'kmaq treaty rights, Indigenous rights, and Mi'kmaq governance. Concise timeline of treaties for Mi'kmaq peoples.
New Brunswick	http://www.nbapc.org/ Website of the New Brunswick Aboriginal Peoples Council, representing 28 000+ Indigenous peoples living off-reserve. Lists departments, services, resources. http://fneii.ca/index.html Website of the First Nation Education Initiative Incorporated, representing 12 First Nation communities in New Brunswick. Educational resources on First Nation schools, programs, achievements. http://www2.gnb.ca/content/gnb/en/departments/aboriginal_affairs.html Provincial government website on Indigenous peoples in New Brunswick. Lists First Nations in New Brunswick and their contact information.
Québec	http://www.gcc.ca/ Website of the Grand Council of the Crees, the political body that represents 18 000+ Cree people in northern Québec. Lists all represented First Nations, their contact information, and latest governance agreements. http://www.creejustice.ca/index.php/ca/resources/agreements Official site of the Department of Justice for the Cree Nation. Includes current government agreements and legislation, and information on their restorative justice program.
Ontario	https://www.ontario.ca/page/treaties Comprehensive site about treaties, relationships, and Indigenous rights in Ontario. Has an abundance of treaty resources from videos and maps to classroom lessons and activities. http://www.Anishinabek.ca/education-resources/ Part of the website of the Union of Ontario Indians representing 40 First Nations in Ontario. Provides many educational kits on treaty education and reconciliation. Videos, lesson plans, maps, and other key resources are featured. http://www.chiefs-of-ontario.org/faq This website link answers/questions about treaties and why they must be honoured. Includes a statement about what understanding First Nation sovereignty means to all peoples.
Manitoba	http://www.trcm.ca/treaty-education-initiative/k-12-treaty-education-continuum/ A webpage of the Treaty Relations Commission of Manitoba with a comprehensive K to 12 treaty curriculum that is a model of breadth, scope, and excellence. Lesson plans with curriculum connections are included.

PROVINCE/ TERRITORY	SUGGESTED RESOURCE WEBSITES
Manitoba (continued)	**https://mfnerc.org/** Website of the Manitoba First Nations Education Resource Centre Inc., a leading educational organization that provides resources and services to First Nation schools. Hosts an amazing video library that showcases communities and culture. **http://umanitoba.ca/nctr/** Website of the National Centre for Truth and Reconciliation in Canada, housed at the University of Manitoba. An iconic resource for information on residential schools, history, and Indigenous resilience.
Saskatchewan	**http://www.otc.ca/** Website for the Office of the Treaty Commissioner, founded by the Federation of Saskatchewan Indians and the Government of Canada. Provides information on treaties and relationships, including an amazing treaty timeline, maps, and the treaties themselves. **https://treaty6education.lskysd.ca** Website for Treaty 6 Education, with engaging and authentic classroom units on Treaty 6. Describes various treaty perspectives and current protocols for working with communities. **http://www.fsin.com/about/** Website of the Federation of Sovereign Indigenous Nations, representing 74 Saskatchewan First Nations and established to protect inherent and treaty rights.
Alberta	**http://treaty8.ca/** Website for the Treaty 8 First Nations and home to 39 First Nations. Represents one of the largest treaty areas in the country (840 000 kilometres). Has cultural, linguistic, and legal information with resources. **http://www.learnalberta.ca/content/aswt/index.html** Website of a not-for-profit learning repository funded by the Government of Alberta. Has digital resources and lessons on Indigenous knowledge and history. **http://www.treatysix.org/** Website for the Confederacy of Treaty Six First Nations, representing 50 First Nations. Includes amazing treaty history and connections to the Royal Proclamation of 1763, along with links to member nations. **http://www.makingtreaty7.com/** Website of the Making Treaty 7 Cultural Society. Provides information on the significance of the treaty, along with educational resources including videos, lesson plans, and voices of youth.
British Columbia	**http://www.fnesc.ca/** Website of the First Nations Education Steering Committee. Provides significant resources on Indigenous peoples, including curriculum units, lesson plans, blogs, key resources on culture, history and language, and professional development opportunities for teachers.

PROVINCE/ TERRITORY	SUGGESTED RESOURCE WEBSITES
British Columbia (continued)	http://www.bctreaty.ca/ Website for the BC Treaty Commission. Includes current information and resources on BC treaties with First Nations. Provides updates on treaty negotiations and why treaties are important, along with an amazing interactive timeline. https://bctf.ca/IssuesInEducation.aspx?id=5684 Website of the British Columbia Teachers' Federation. Offers concise information on understanding treaties and the treaty process, as well as clear descriptions of the implications of treaties for all citizens.
Yukon	http://www.yesnet.yk.ca/firstnations/ Part of the website for the Yukon Education Student Network. An extensive resource about Yukon First Nations' history, culture, and languages. Includes a curriculum link with lessons and units for K to 12. https://cyfn.ca/ Website of the Council of Yukon First Nations, with the most up-to-date information on land claims and issues. Detailed descriptions of the history and languages of Yukon, along with links to Yukon First Nations. http://www.gov.yk.ca/aboutyukon/peopleandplaces.html Website of the Government of Yukon, with a good introduction to Yukon First Nations. Includes maps and descriptions of Yukon Indigenous languages.
Northwest Territories	http://denenation.com/ Website of the Dene Nation in Northwest Territories. Includes information and resources on history (timeline), lands and environment, and communities. Extensive bank of images of Dene peoples. https://www.eia.gov.nt.ca/en/priorities/meeting-gnwts-legal-duty-consult-aboriginal-governments Website of Executive and Indigenous Affairs, Government of Northwest Territories. Provides quick links to land claim and self-government agreements, as well as current negotiations (including transboundary negotiations with bordering First Nations and the federal government).
Nunavut	http://www.gov.nu.ca/ Website of the Government of Nunavut. Includes extensive resources on culture, language, and history, as well as detailed community profiles. http://www.polarnet.ca/polarnet/nunavut.htm Website of PolarNet, a communications company run by Indigenous peoples. Offers a concise summary of the Nunavut Agreement and provides links to online regional newspapers. http://nunavuttourism.com/about-nunavut/people-of-nunavut Website of Nunavut Tourism. Offers concise information about Nunavut and its 4000-year occupation by Indigenous peoples, along with links to Nunavut culture and an interactive map.

WAMPUM BELTS, SACRED SCROLLS, ARTIFACTS, AND ORAL HISTORY

Many of the agreements, history, and traditions of Indigenous peoples have been recorded in the form of wampum belts, sacred scrolls, artifacts – including pictographs, petroglyphs, totem poles, and drums – and complex knowledge systems.

TOTEM POLES IN THE PACIFIC NORTHWEST

Figure 3.2. Kwakiutl totem pole from Campbell River, British Columbia.

Carved of large, straight, red cedar and painted vibrant colours, the totem pole is emblematic of West Coast Indigenous culture. There are six principal types of poles: memorial or heraldic poles, grave figures, house posts, house front or portal poles, welcoming poles, and mortuary poles. Completed totem poles are usually erected as part of potlatch ceremonies and depict crest animals such as the beaver, killer whale, and raven. These crest animals are the property of specific family lineages and reflect the history of that lineage. Totem poles naturally weathered over time in the wet coastal climate and were allowed to decay and fall.

Wampum Belts

Wampum belts, used mainly by Indigenous peoples of the Eastern Woodlands, are sacred and represent "a person's credentials or a certificate of authority" at political and religious events (Haudenosaunee Confederacy 2017, 1). Each wampum belt is accompanied by a highly trained and skilled interpreter or wampum keeper who is entrusted with these historical records.

WHAT IS WAMPUM?

The word *wampum* – from a Narragansett (Algonquian language family) word meaning "a string of white shell beads" – is used for the tubular white and purple beads made from Atlantic coast seashells (usually whelk shell for white beads and quahog clam shell for purple). Belts made of wampum were used to mark agreements between peoples, especially treaties and covenants made between Indigenous peoples and European colonial powers.

Figure 3.3. Wampum belt from the Eastern Woodlands region.

Sacred Scrolls

Many Indigenous nations in North America had written histories in the form of sacred scrolls and other objects (Haudenosaunee Confederacy 2017; Office of the Treaty Commissioners 2017). These etched scrolls often contained mnemonic, or memory-aiding, symbols. They were always accompanied by an Indigenous expert who was a keeper of that artifact and its oral history, and was highly trained in interpreting it. For example, the sacred scrolls kept by Ojibwe spiritual leaders documented the ceremonies, history, and worldview of their nation. They reflected the depth of Ojibwe teachings and values through symbols that could range from relatively simple to extremely complex.

As with wampum belts, sacred scrolls were used to record the history or mark a significant event in the lives of Indigenous peoples. Some scrolls recorded how particular traditional ceremonies were to be organized. Among Ojibwe peoples, some scrolls documented the migration of the Anishinaabek from the east coast of Canada to Madeline Island in Lake Superior. The sacred scroll in figure 3.4 is only one out of more than one hundred that were examined by researcher Selwyn Dewdney.

Figure 3.4. Image of a birchbark scroll

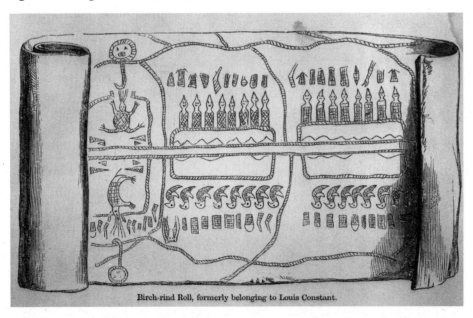

Birch-rind Roll, formerly belonging to Louis Constant.

A reproduction of a portion of a birchbark scroll from the Midewiwin (Grand Medicine) society of the Ojibwe peoples. The scroll depicts several interconnected lodges, members, and practices.

Truth and Reconciliation in Canadian Schools

Petroglyphs and Pictographs

Petroglyphs and pictographs are other examples of how Indigenous peoples documented significant events in their own lives and that of their communities (Bradshaw Foundation 2017). Petroglyphs are carvings in rock, while pictographs are paintings on rock, typically done with red ochre or another natural dye. These unique art forms provide a glimpse into Indigenous spirituality, dreams, and history. They are found across the country from Kejimkujik National Park (Nova Scotia) and the Qajartalik petroglyph site (Eastern Arctic) to Writing-On-Stone Provincial Park (Alberta) and Nanaimo Petroglyph Park (Vancouver Island, British Columbia).

As with the wampum belts and sacred scrolls, petroglyphs and pictographs are considered sacred, connected to the land and the people. Because of these ongoing sacred connections, entering into treaties was not taken lightly by Indigenous peoples. They came to the treaty table with a particular lens and worldview that viewed all as sacred. Treaties were not seen as a secular act focused on individualism and cessation of lands and identity (which was the view of the Crown at the time of treaty signings).

Figure 3.5. Tracings of pictographs in a glacial erratic cave, Nanton, Alberta.

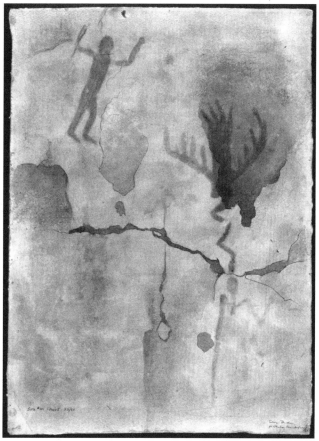

WHY SOCIAL STUDIES, HISTORY, GEOGRAPHY, AND CANADIAN AND WORLD STUDIES ARE AN IDEAL APPROACH TO TEACHING ABOUT TREATIES

Treaties are living documents that were signed between nations, as well as primary historical sources. These formal agreements have comprehensive implications today. The concept that "we are all treaty people" applies to all Canadians and residents (Office of the Treaty Commissioner 2017). Examining treaties as part of a process of historical inquiry offers students an opportunity to question, gather evidence (primary and secondary artifacts), and consider various perspectives (Stanford History Education Group 2017). The beauty of history, embedded with inquiry, is that it has the potential to build bridges between the past, present, and future. It also gives students the chance to engage in new ways of relating to Indigenous peoples. Table 3.2 provides educators with suggested materials, activities, and curriculum connections for exploring treaties, treaty relationships, and Indigenous connections to their lands.

Table 3.2. Social Studies, History, Geography, and Canadian and World Studies Curriculum Connections and Resources

CURRICULUM CONNECTIONS	SUGGESTED BOOKS/TEXTS BY GRADE
Primary (K to 3)	
K – Belonging and Contributing – While reading *A Circle of Friends,* encourage students to talk about their own families, heritage, and culture. Extend this conversation by having students discuss similarities and differences with Indigenous peoples from the story.	**K** – *A Circle of Friends* by Penny Terry Mack (2012)
1 – The Local Community – After reading *T Is for Territories: A Yukon, Northwest Territories and Nunavut Alphabet,* guide students in a discussion about what makes these territories unique. Extend this discussion by having students identify some of the natural and built features in these communities. Compare areas.	**1** – *T Is for Territories: A Yukon, Northwest Territories and Nunavut Alphabet* by Michael Kusugak (2013)
2 – Changing Family and Community Traditions – Read *Two Row Wampum.* Discuss the importance of this tradition among the Haudenosaunee. Extend this conversation by encouraging students to connect with their own celebrations and traditions, and discussing potential reasons for change.	**2** – *Two Row Wampum* by Michelle Corneau (2016)
3 – Communities in Canada, 1780–1850 – While reading *Eagle Feather: An Honour,* ask students to describe how First Nations view their Elders. Extend this discussion by linking this conversation to life in 1850 and the values Indigenous peoples possessed (and those that still continue today).	**3** – *Eagle Feather: An Honour* by Ferguson Plain (1989)

Truth and Reconciliation in Canadian Schools

CURRICULUM CONNECTIONS	SUGGESTED BOOKS/TEXTS BY GRADE

Junior (4 to 6)

4 – Political and Physical Regions of Canada – While reading *Idaa Trail: In the Steps of Our Ancestors,* ask students to describe these traditional lands and the original peoples who live on them. Extend this conversation by comparing their own locations to that of the Dogrib (Tłîchô).

5 – The Role of Government and Responsible Citizenship – Go to the section on Nunavut in *The 10 Most Significant Crossroads in Aboriginal History,* and complete the activities listed. Extend this activity by discussing this new form of government.

6 – Communities in Canada, Past and Present – Review the sections related to treaties in *We Are All Treaty People* in a concise and chronological manner. Ask students to describe how these critical developments affected the history of First Nations and settlers.

4 – *Idaa Trail: In the Steps of Our Ancestors* by Wendy Stephenson (2005)

5 – *The 10 Most Significant Crossroads in Aboriginal History* by Jan Beaver (2008)

6 – *We Are All Treaty People* by Maurice Switzer (2011)

Intermediate (7 and 8)

7 – New France and British North America, 1713–1800 – Complete the intermediate treaty activities in *Aboriginal History and Realities in Canada.* Extend this activity by focusing on the political and legal changes during these times and discussing what these changes mean for Indigenous and non-Indigenous lives today.

8 – Global Settlement: Patterns and Sustainability – Review the treaty negotiation section in Unit 2 of *Aboriginal Peoples: Building for the Future,* and complete the suggested activities. Extend this activity by identifying land issues and the responses of various groups in Canada. Compare this situation to another Indigenous nation elsewhere in the world.

7 – *Aboriginal History and Realities in Canada* by the Elementary Teachers' Federation of Ontario (2015)

8 – *Aboriginal Peoples: Building for the Future* by Kevin Reed (1999)

Secondary (9 to 12)

9 – Issues in Canadian Geography – Select and complete activities on treaties from the Sovereignty and Self-Determination section in *Aboriginal Beliefs, Values and Aspirations.* Extend this activity by connecting students' findings to characteristics and patterns of land use in these treaty territories in Canada.

10 – Civics and Citizenship – Read Chapter 5 in *The Ruptured Sky: The War of 1812.* Closely review the historical timeline of significant events. Connect this content to the civic actions of Indigenous peoples and how these nations made a difference in the establishment of Canada.

9 – *Aboriginal Beliefs, Values and Aspirations* by Kevin Reed, Natasha Beeds, Mary Joy Elijah, Keith Lickers and Neal McLeod (2011)

10 – *The Ruptured Sky: The War of 1812* (print/digital) (2013)

CURRICULUM CONNECTIONS	SUGGESTED BOOKS/TEXTS BY GRADE
11 – Politics in Action – Select and complete activities on treaties from the governance section in *Aboriginal Peoples in Canada*. Extend this activity by connecting students' findings to the recent key changes in Canadian law and policy that treaties have brought about. Examine what the implications are for Indigenous and non-Indigenous citizens alike.	**11** – *Aboriginal Peoples in Canada* by Kevin Reed, Natasha Beeds, Mary Joy Elijah, Keith Lickers, and Neal McLeod (2011)
12 – History, Identity, and Culture – Review key content on treaties in Chapters 26 through 28 from *Indigenous Writes: A Guide to First Nations, Métis & Inuit Issues in Canada*. Extend this activity by connecting to themes of diversity and citizenship, especially in the way treaties and land claims are at the forefront of issues in Canada today.	**12** – *Indigenous Writes: A Guide to First Nations, Métis & Inuit Issues in Canada* by Chelsea Vowel (2016)

The curriculum connections in this table come from modified versions of specific expectations in the Ontario curriculum (elementary social studies, history, and geography, and secondary Canadian and world studies courses).

CONCLUSION

The Ontario Treaties Recognition Act (2016) is the first legislation of its kind in Canada that provides a "recurring opportunity for teachers to plan learning activities about treaties during the school year" (Government of Ontario 2017, 1). In 2016, Ontario marked its first Treaties Recognition Week from November 6 to 12. This commitment to treaty education strengthens a greatly needed awareness that "we are all treaty people," an important concept for Indigenous and non-Indigenous citizens alike. The many benefits that Canadians enjoy are the result of treaties, as well as the continuous sacrifices made by the original peoples of this land.

I hope that similar legislation and/or a binding commitment to treaty education is introduced in all provinces and territories. Understanding treaties is essential for reconciliation with and appreciation of the Indigenous peoples of Canada.

Chapter 4. Contributions of Indigenous Peoples

Call 62.i. – Education for Reconciliation (TRC Calls to Action)

"We call upon the federal, provincial, and territorial governments, in consultation and collaboration with Survivors, Aboriginal peoples, and educators, to make age-appropriate curriculum on … Aboriginal peoples' historical and contemporary contributions to Canada."

INTRODUCTION

When I went to elementary and secondary school, little or nothing was taught about the contributions of Indigenous peoples to the world. A couple of decades later, I find myself witnessing a movement where the First Nation, Métis, and Inuit worldview is being embedded in the K to 12 curriculum. It is often overwhelming for me to think that all students (regardless of ancestry) will begin to learn about the truth, diversity, and beauty of Indigenous nations. This learning has always been a crucial step in promoting understanding and building relationships between students. I am so moved by the fact that my nephews, nieces, and future family members will have the opportunity to stand proud when our contributions become common knowledge for all.

The Calls to Action in the Truth and Reconciliation Commission of Canada (TRC) final report provide practical recommendations for education for reconciliation by "mak[ing] age-appropriate curriculum on … Aboriginal peoples' historical and contemporary contributions to Canada" (TRC 2015, 331) a priority. This chapter therefore embraces that particular Call to Action and provides a space for the innovations and inventions of Indigenous peoples to come alive.

As we continue our journey together, I ask you, the reader, to reflect on the following facts.

- Over 500 diverse Indigenous nations in North America (Turtle Island) gave many agricultural, medical, aquacultural, metallurgical, pharmacological, and scientific contributions to the world (Keoke and Porterfield 2002).
- More than 7000 Indigenous peoples participated in World War I, World War II, and the Korean War (representing the largest enrollment per capita by cultural group) to protect the rights and freedoms enjoyed by Canadians (Lackenbauer, Moses, Sheffield & Gohier, n.d.).

- The Métis are often known as the "founders of the fur trade" and served key roles as interpreters, boat operators, traders, guides, and voyageurs, as well as being the first postmen in Canada (Barkwell 2017, 1).
- The Inuit parka and boots (traditionally made with caribou or sealskin and sinew) continue to influence the design of winter clothing around the world (The Inuit Impact/ Inuit Cultural Online Resource 2017).

TURTLE ISLAND AND INDIGENOUS TRADITIONAL LANDS

What is Turtle Island? Where is it? And why do so many Indigenous nations in North America call their lands by this name?

All of the more than 500 nations have creation stories that retell ancestral understandings of how their worlds came to be (Toulouse 2016a). Each of these stories fosters a community's continued connection to the Earth and all her children (ibid.). Part of the Ojibwe peoples' creation story details the sacrifice of one brave muskrat that dived to the bottom of the ocean to grab a handful of earth. This earth was then placed on the back of a turtle and the original human being blew the life breath of the Creator onto this earth. From this sacred act, the continent of North America was born.

The Haudenosaunee creation story also depicts the establishment of land on the back of a turtle in the legend of Sky Woman, a beautiful woman who lived on an island in the sky. She dropped from her home in the air and was gently guided down onto the back of a turtle by the animals that lived on Earth. The water animals, Beaver and Otter, worked to prepare a home for her by grabbing mud from the bottom of the ocean, and placing it on the turtle's back. This mud grew and grew and became the traditional lands of the Haudenosaunee peoples.

These ancient narratives on how things came to be provide insight into the term *Turtle Island,* but they also reveal Indigenous peoples' intimate connection to stewardship. These two creation stories, like all other such stories, are deeply rooted in Indigenous languages, traditions, and worldview. Turtle Island is more than a place that is today known as North America. For Indigenous peoples it is, and always will be, home.

The original lands of Indigenous peoples can be understood in many ways. As a means of organizing the material, we will look at Turtle Island through a geographic lens. Figure 4.1 depicts our shared continent separated into 12 distinct areas.

Each of these 12 areas is unique in its climate, land features, flora, fauna, and other key geographic features. The Indigenous peoples who lived in these areas learned how to work with their surroundings to survive and thrive. They had to apply their ingenuity to the struggles and challenges posed by that particular habitat, resulting in key innovations and inventions. The myth that the people stereotypically known as Indians (as popularized by one-dimensional westerns) had no forms of technology is entirely false (First Nations Child & Family Caring Society of Canada 2016). The breechcloth-wearing and tipi-living images that saturated North American pop culture (and mindsets) denied non-Indigenous citizens the right to know the truth about the original peoples.

Figure 4.1. Twelve Traditional Geographic Land Areas of Indigenous Peoples

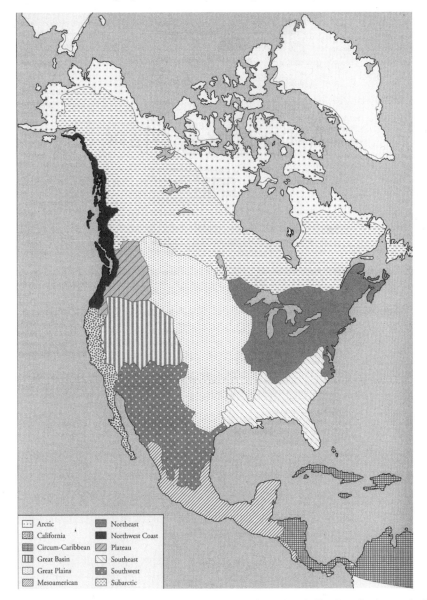

This map has been adapted from Keoke and Porterfield's *Encyclopedia of American Indian Contributions to the World* (2002).

The 500-plus nations living in these distinct geographic land areas have given so many gifts to the world. They range from pharmaceutical innovations to sports and games to surgical and agricultural techniques, musical instruments, and much more. Many of the foods we enjoy come from Indigenous peoples (Indigenous and Northern Affairs Canada 2017), and many of the continent's place names come from their languages. So many gifts and yet so few people in Canada know about their origins.

In Table 4.1, I offer a small sample of those contributions and challenge you, the reader, to identify ones that are part of your life today.

Figure 4.1. Indigenous Contributions by Geographic Land Area

GEOGRAPHIC LAND AREA	SELECT CONTRIBUTIONS
Arctic	crampons, flotation devices, portable space heaters, kayaks, shovels, snowshoes, trousers (two fur leggings sewn together with a seam in the front and the rear)
California	asphalt, detergents, forest management, hair conditioners, stretchers, chewing gum, chemical fishing (the scrapings of certain yam roots were placed on the surface of a lake to stun the nervous systems of fish when eaten)
Circum-Caribbean	barbeques, camouflage, musical instruments, pottery, fishhooks, cigars, hammocks
Great Basin	laminated bows, oral contraception, ephedra, medication, insecticides, asepsis (use of balsam, known as "cough root," to disinfect an area for surgery or medical treatment), chia sage (salvia columbariae, used for both medicine and food)
Great Plains	astronomy, deodorant, footbags (currently known as "hacky sacks"), military tactics, seed selection, sign language, tipis
Mesoamerica	aqueducts, basketball, shipping canals, twist-on jar lids, cocoa, skin grafts, umbrellas
Northeast	anesthetics, copper axes, bunk beds, potato chips, hockey (ice and field), lacrosse, petroleum jelly
Northwest Coast	anatomical knowledge, architects, boxes, hemostats (tools used in surgery to control bleeding), x-ray art, needles, jackstraws (game played with strips of wood or bone)
Plateau	decoy ducks, embroidery, fringed clothing, looms, plant classification, Appaloosa horse breed, cascara sagrada (bark of the California buckthorn used as a laxative and tonic)
Southeast	arthritis treatments, briquettes, calendars, civic centres, evaporative cooling, irrigation systems, seawalls
Southwest	apartment complexes, basketball, chiles, surgical drainage, turquoise jewellery, seed selection, xeriscaping (using plants that can tolerate drought conditions or do not require additional watering)
Subarctic	cradleboards, cranberries, dogsleds, home insulation, parkas, insect bite remedies, cat's cradle (a string game)

These innovations and inventions are only a sample from the Indigenous nations in these areas (Keoke and Porterfield 2003).

SPECIFIC CONTRIBUTIONS OF FIRST NATION, INUIT, AND MÉTIS PEOPLES

First Nations

One of my favourite childhood memories is of our family farm on Sagamok First Nation. We spent many days there weeding potato plants, picking potatoes, and helping take care of the sugar bush. My grandfather William and his buddy Neonse would pack all the kids up and take us to the farm to work. My cousins and I would turn the day into lots of fun and laughter (besides hard work). On one of those summer days, I ended up with a bleeding nose that would not stop. At age seven, I was scared because there was so much blood. My cousins took me to my grandfather, who immediately picked a cluster of tiny white flowers that smelled strongly like pepper (called "yarrow" or *Achillea millefolium*). He shoved the flowers into my nostrils, and within two minutes the bleeding stopped. What I learned that day was to appreciate the medical knowledge that my grandfather possessed. It was immediate, natural, and safe. My view on medicine and health was forever changed by that experience.

EUROPEAN SETTLERS ON THE WEST COAST

On the West Coast, the relationship between European settlers and the region's First Nations inhabitants developed quite differently from that between settlers and First Nations in the Great Lakes basin. The first settlement in present-day British Columbia was built in territory of the Nuu-chah-nulth people of Nootka Sound on the west coast of Vancouver Island. Santa Cruz de Nuca was a Spanish settlement and the first European colony in British Columbia. Established in 1789, it existed until 1795 when it was abandoned following the Nootka Crisis that almost led to war between Britain and Spain.

Another gift of First Nation peoples was the extension of real friendship to settler cultures on Turtle Island. The newcomers could not have survived without Indigenous peoples' generosity (TRC 2015). For example, methods and techniques for transportation on land and water were shared with settlers.

First Nations were often the first contact that non-Indigenous peoples had in North America, whether it was the Haida on the west coast or the Mi'kmaq on the east. Because their contributions helped build this country, the time for real recognition is overdue.

Figure 4.2. Traditional Canoe of the Ojibwe

Indigenous nations had various forms of land and water transportation. This canoe, from the Ojibwe peoples, is one example. Canoes like these were commonly used in the fur trade in Canada.

Many place names in our country have First Nations origins: Niagara, Gaspé, Nipissing, Kamloops, Mississauga, Winnipeg, Athabasca, Ottawa, Toronto, and Nanaimo are only a few of them. In fact, almost 30 000 official Canadian place names in 84 Indigenous languages or dialects are of Indigenous origin (Natural Resources Canada 2017). Our country's name comes from the Wendat (Huron) peoples, whose original word for "the village" (*kanata*) eventually became "Canada." My people, the Anishinaabek, have a similar word to describe the traditional lands of the Ojibwe. Elder Merle Assance-Beedie shared with me the word *kinadeh* (pronounced like "Canada") and gave a beautiful explanation of its meaning. Kinadeh comes from two syllables: *kina* and *deh*. *Kina* means "everything you see around you," while *deh* refers to "the heart." It is an Ojibwe teaching that the heart comes directly from our Creator. Therefore, kinadeh means "everything you see around you has the heart of the Creator." Merle has been in the Spirit World for a number of years now, but her teachings and her understanding of the language continue to have an impact on my work today.

I experience a level of anxiety when I talk about other Indigenous nations, especially when they are not Ojibwe (my own roots). Like me, many educators are afraid of getting the Indigenous worldview wrong (Snively & Williams 2016). However, I am not fearful of saying that I do not know and I am trying to find ways to do better. I too want to get things right and be honourable.

Inuit

When I teach about other Indigenous nations, I often draw on primary and secondary resources that have been critically vetted. I also like to focus on the inventions and innovations of those nations as a different way to explore this cultural knowledge (Toulouse 2016a). For me, it feels like a safe entry point in discussing that nation, especially if a member of that community is not available.

As an example, I have very limited connections to Inuit peoples, but I have deep respect for their ways of knowing. They possess a level of creativity in response to their surroundings that is beyond my imagination. For example, Inuit snow goggles are not only practical, but aesthetically stunning as well. Figure 4.3 shows a set of traditional snow goggles that are the coolest sunglasses ever created. They were usually made from ivory or wood.

While driving along highways in Canada, I often see rock sculptures at the side of the road that emulate the Inuit inuksuk. I am sure you have seen them, as well. You might even have tried building these unique constructions. Inuksuit (plural for inuksuk) are "stone marker[s] that act in the place of a person" (The Inuit Impact/Inuit Cultural Online Resource 2017, 1). These figures have been used for thousands of years by Inuit and other peoples of the Arctic region of North America for hunting, navigation, and as message centres. Inuksuit have become global symbols of Canada and the north.

Figure 4.3. Traditional Inuit Snow Goggles

These snow goggles were made from wood and sinew. They were used to prevent snow blindness.

Truth and Reconciliation in Canadian Schools

The Inuit have contributed to the global identity of Canada in many other ways. Beyond the familiar kayak and parka are internationally known individuals such as Sheila Watt-Cloutier, International Chair for the Inuit Circumpolar Conference and nominee for the Nobel Peace Prize; Jordin Tootoo, the first Inuk to play in the NHL; and Susan Aglukark, recording artist and recipient of several Juno awards (ibid.). I challenge you to discover more of these Inuit contributions with your students.

Métis

Many of my friends are Métis, and I live in an area where there is a strong Métis presence. My husband, Luc, who has Indigenous roots, is also Métis. The university where I currently work celebrates Indigenous peoples, and our Métis community is quite large. I feel very privileged to experience the diversity in culture that Métis peoples possess. There is a connection based in pride of ancestry and the gift of humour that binds us all together. Métis contributions to the establishment of Canada cannot be underestimated. Their ancestors guaranteed the success of the fur trade (Métis Culture/Our Legacy 2017), and their creation of the Red River cart (figure 4.4) demonstrates their resourcefulness.

Figure 4.4. Traditional Métis Cart

This cart, made of wood and leather, was buoyant, and could carry up to 450 kilograms across land and water.

The ever-evolving Métis nation was born during the 17th century. Emerging from the marriages of European traders and First Nations' women, this highly diverse community has continued to grow. Representatives of the Hudson's Bay Company (HBC) described Métis men as easily identifiable "by a blue capote (coat), beaded pipe bag and bright red L'Assomption sash" (ibid., 3). The language known as Michif (a complex blend of French, Cree, and Ojibwe) was widely spoken by the Métis and is now undergoing a resurgence.

Historically, the Métis were strongly associated with the North West Company (NWC), a fur-trading entity in competition with the HBC. In a gift-giving ceremony in 1814, NWC partner Alexander MacDonell presented the Métis with a flag featuring a white horizonal figure eight, or infinity symbol, on a blue background. Two years later, the flag – with a red background rather than blue – was carried by the Métis in a conflict after the Governor of Assiniboia prohibited the Métis from selling their goods and using horses to hunt bison (Barkwell 2017; Métis Culture/Our Legacy 2017). This prohibition led to a conflict in which 21 settlers and one Métis were killed.

WHAT DOES THE INFINITY SYMBOL MEAN?

As a symbol of nationhood, the Métis flag predates Canada's maple leaf flag by about 150 years.

For Métis, the white infinity symbol has two meanings: the joining of two cultures, and the existence of a people forever. Some Métis believe the symbol is based on the Plains Indian sign language for the Red River carts used by the Métis: two circles with the thumbs and forefingers joined and the hands held together. The more common interpretation is that the flag is based on the flag of Scotland with its white diagonal cross and blue background. The Métis flag is carried today as a symbol of continuity and pride.

The Métis have made many contributions to Canadian culture and society. They invented the York boat that was used on large bodies of water and could carry six tonnes of cargo, and made fishing a "year-round commercial industry with the ingenious 'jigger' that was used to set nets under the ice" (Barkwell 2017, 1). They also invented pemmican, a mix of bison meat, wild berries, and wild vegetables that became a food staple in the 18th century and is the basis for jerky and dried foods today. They added the art of fiddle music and jigging (a form of dancing) to the Canadian identity (Métis Culture/Our Legacy 2017). They also served in many international conflicts, including the War of 1812, the Boer War, both world wars, and the Korean War (Lackenbauer et al., n.d.).

The women of the Métis Nation come from long lines of strong and resilient ancestors. Their flower beadwork, unique histories, and knowledge of their culture continue to influence the sustainability of their people. Métis women were the foundation of the fur trade. They were able to translate Cree and Ojibwe for their husbands in any conflicts that arose, and they were the bridge between European and Indigenous peoples in their trade relations.

ANISHINAABEK, MUSHKEGOWUK, AND HAUDENOSAUNEE CONTRIBUTIONS

Ontario is now home to many Indigenous nations; however, the Anishinaabek, Mushkegowuk, and Haudenosaunee peoples have lived there since time immemorial. Who are they? And what innovations are they known for?

Truth and Reconciliation in Canadian Schools

The Anishinaabek are made up of Odawa, Ojibwe, Pottawatomi, Mississauga, and Algonquin peoples. They have resided around the Great Lakes (especially Lake Huron, Lake Superior, and Lake Michigan) for thousands of years, as well as parts of the Subarctic and Plains. The Mushkegowuk are the Cree peoples. They have lived in the James Bay and Hudson Bay areas, plus a large portion of the Subarctic and Plains, for many millennia. The Haudenosaunee include the Mohawk, Oneida, Onondaga, Tuscarora, Seneca, and Cayuga peoples. They have always lived around specific waterways like the Great Lakes, especially Lake Ontario and Lake Erie, the Grand River, and several wide areas around Niagara.

Table 4.2. Select Anishinaabek, Mushkegowuk, and Haudenosaunee Contributions

NATION	INNOVATIONS	SELECT INNOVATION
Anishinaabek	maple syrup, megaphones, moccasins, shovels, obstetrics, soft drink ingredients	**Soft drink ingredients** Soda water taken from mineral springs was often combined with sassafras, wintergreen, and birch to create a root beer-like drink. This drink also had several medicinal qualities and was used as a tonic. Its ingredients were the inspiration for Dr. Pepper.
Mushkegowuk	botanical mints, persimmons, three-pole tipis, toboggans, walking out ceremonies for children, Idle No More Indigenous rights movement (then-Chief Theresa Spence of the Attawapiskat First Nation declared a hunger strike to focus attention on First Nations issues)	**Walking out ceremonies for children** This ceremony is a traditional welcoming of the child to Cree society. A tent is set up with the doorway facing east. A short path from the tent to a small decorated tree is prepared. The infant is guided from the tent doorway and around the tree and back to the tent. The child then gives a variety of gifts to the Elders.
Haudenosaunee	The Three Sisters (corn, beans, squash), lacrosse, women's rights, astringents, petroleum, influence on United States constitution of 1789 (the Haudenosaunee Great Law of Peace has been dated by historians at 1450, but the Haudenosaunee place it between 1000 and 1400)	**The Three Sisters** Corn, beans, and squash were the three main agricultural crops of the Haudenosaunee (and others), always planted as a trio because they thrive together, much like three inseparable sisters. Together, the sisters provide a balanced diet from a single planting. When European settlers arrived in North America in the early 1600s, the Haudenosaunee had been growing the three sisters for over three centuries.

This table shows only a small selection of the gifts that these nations gave to the world. It is important to connect with the communities themselves to explore these and other contributions.

Source: Keoke and Porterfield, *American Indian Contributions to the World: 15 000 Years of Inventions and Innovations* (2002).

The Anishinaabek, Mushkegowuk, and Haudenosaunee peoples are highly diverse in the breadth of their contributions, languages, and worldview. I suggest conducting your own research into these nations by beginning with these websites:

- http://www.anishinabek.ca/
  Website of Anishinabek Nation/Union of Ontario Indians, the political advocate for 40 Anishinaabek First Nations
- http://www.haudenosauneeconfederacy.com/
  Official website of the Haudenosaunee Confederacy
- http://www.mushkegowuk.com/
  Website for seven Mushkegowuk nations in the western James Bay and Hudson Bay areas
- https://www.aiai.on.ca/
  Website for the Association of Iroquois and Allied Indians in Ontario
- http://www.chiefs-of-ontario.org/
  Website for the secretariat advocating for 133 First Nations in Ontario
- http://www.ofifc.org/
  Website for the Ontario Federation of Indian Friendship Centres
- http://www.edu.gov.on.ca/eng/aboriginal/
  Website for the Indigenous Education Strategy of the Ontario Ministry of Education

The preceding list is only a starting point and is not meant to be exhaustive. It is always crucial to begin with the nations in your area.

WHY SCIENCE IS AN IDEAL APPROACH TO TEACHING ABOUT INDIGENOUS CONTRIBUTIONS

Snively and Williams (2016), in their book *Knowing Home: Braiding Indigenous Science with Western Science,* capture the essence of why it is essential to adopt a more holistic approach to teaching science in schools. Current science education can often be "neither personally meaningful nor useful to [students'] everyday lives" (Snively & Williams 2016, 1). Indigenous learners need an authentic connection that reinforces their cultures, traditions, and ways of knowing. This is one reason why I have selected science as a subject for this chapter (combined with Indigenous literature on innovations/inventions).

Table 4.3 offers ideas on how to connect science in K to 12 classrooms with the suggested books on Indigenous contributions. These texts have been vetted by various sources and are level appropriate. The science connections for each resource focus on a particular curricular strand that can be further explored with students.

Table 4.3. Science Curriculum Connections and Resources

CURRICULUM CONNECTIONS	SUGGESTED BOOKS BY GRADE
Primary (K to 3)	
K – Problem Solving and Innovating – While listening to the book *Thirteen Moons on Turtle's Back: A Native American Year of Moons,* ask students to identify the specialized vocabulary (e.g., cycles, moons, seasons). Encourage students to discuss these moons and the seasons that they occur in. **1 – Materials, Objects, and Everyday Structures** – While reading *The Métis Alphabet Book,* ask students to identify objects in the book they also have at home and/or at school (e.g., mittens, fiddle). Discuss the differences in the materials. **2 – Growth and Changes in Animals** – Before reading *Giveaways: An ABC Book of Loanwords from the Americas,* have students identify the animals on the cover. After reading the book, add to the list of animals recognized. Describe the physical characteristics of select animals. **3 – Forces Causing Movement** – Select one of the bowl or ball games from *Native American Games and Stories.* Read the short story about that game and play it. With your students, discuss the forces that caused that object to start, stop, and change direction (e.g., bats, balls, hands, bowls).	K – *Thirteen Moons on Turtle's Back: A Native American Year of Moons* by Joseph Bruchac and Jonathon London (1997) 1 – *The Métis Alphabet Book* by Joseph Jean Fauchon (2009) 2 – *Giveaways: An ABC Book of Loanwords from the Americas* by Linda Boyden (2010) 3 – *Native American Games and Stories* by James Bruchac and Joe Bruchac (2000)
Junior (4 to 6)	
4 – Habitats and Communities – Select the Indigenous cultural region in Canada from *The Kids Book of Aboriginal Peoples in Canada* that applies to your area (the book also includes the political divisions of provinces/territories). Review that region and identify the factors that contribute to and affect the survival of plants and animals in your area. **5 – Conservation of Energy and Resources** – Review the section on shelters in *A Native American Thought of It: Amazing Inventions and Innovations.* Ask students to think about how the designs of these structures were efficient in their particular environments (e.g., wigwams in northern Ontario, hogans in the desert, plank houses on the west coast). **6 – Biodiversity** – Select for review one of the sections on food or medicine and healing from *The Inuit Thought of It: Amazing Arctic Innovations.* Ask students to identify products (and their sources) that contribute to Inuit life. Extend this activity by discussing interconnectedness among species (e.g., plant, animal, human).	4 – *The Kids Book of Aboriginal Peoples in Canada* by Diane Silvey (2012) 5 – *A Native American Thought of It: Amazing Inventions and Innovations* by Rocky Landon and David Macdonald (2008) 6 – *The Inuit Thought of It: Amazing Arctic Innovations* by Alootook Ipellie (2007)

Intermediate (7 and 8)

7 – Form and Function – As you are reading *The Scout: Tommy Prince,* identify the structures that are present (e.g., signs, buildings, statue) in this graphic story. Organize these into solid, frame, and shell structures. Extend this activity by describing the structure (e.g., stability, symmetry, materials) of the Tommy Prince statue.

8 – Systems in Action – Go to the Entries by Subject section in *American Indian Contributions to the World* (paperback). Have students select one innovation and go to that page in the text. Ask them to identify the processes and components that allowed this innovation to work for Indigenous peoples. Extend this activity by comparing this innovation to a similar one today.

7 – *The Scout: Tommy Prince* by David Alexander Robertson (2014)

8 – *American Indian Contributions to the World* (paperback) by Emory Dean Keoke and Kay Marie Porterfield (2003)

Secondary (9 to 12)

9 – Scientific Investigation Skills and Career Exploration – Go to the section on Public Buildings and Cities in *Buildings, Clothing and Art: American Indian Contributions to the World.* Have students formulate questions about the complexity (or simplicity) of these civic centres. Explore the relationships, issues, and ideas that were foundational to these sites.

10 – Physics, Light, and Geometric Optics – Go to the section on Sound and Light in *Science and Technology: American Indian Contributions to the World.* Identify the Indigenous knowledge and technologies related to light. Extend this activity by exploring how these scientific insights and innovations enhanced Indigenous life.

11 – Physics, Forces – Go to the section on Transportation on Water or Transportation on Land in *Trade, Transportation and Warfare: American Indian Contributions to the World.* Have students select one of these Indigenous technologies and explore Newton's laws of force (contact and action-at-a-distance) in relation to this technology.

12 – Chemistry, Organic Chemistry – Go to any one of the three sections on plant medicines in *Medicine and Health: American Indian Contributions to the World.* Have students select one of these medicines and identify the compounds in it. Extend this activity by exploring how similar modern medicines (and their compounds) can be harmful to the environment (e.g., ending up in the water table through improper disposal). Examine ways to provide medicines that leave a healthier footprint on the Earth.

9 – *Buildings, Clothing and Art: American Indian Contributions to the World* by Emory Dean Keoke and Kay Marie Porterfield (2005)

10 – *Science and Technology: American Indian Contributions to the World* by Emory Dean Keoke and Kay Marie Porterfield (2005)

11 – *Trade, Transportation and Warfare: American Indian Contributions to the World* by Emory Dean Keoke and Kay Marie Porterfield (2005)

12 – *Medicine and Health: American Indian Contributions to the World* by Emory Dean Keoke and Kay Marie Porterfield (2005)

The curriculum connections in this table come from modified versions of specific expectations in the Ontario curriculum (elementary science and secondary science courses). These strands engage students with a particular book in a variety of ways.

CONCLUSION

I am a very proud Ojibwe/Odawa woman. My mom, Dorothy Hope Recollet, came from Wikwemikong (Manitoulin Island, Ontario) and was Odawa. My dad, William Nelson Toulouse, comes from Sagamok First Nation, which is on the north shore of Lake Huron (Ontario). He is Ojibwe and a fluent speaker of Anishinaabemowin, possessing a high level of comprehension, speaking ability, and understanding of our traditional language.

My mom has been in the Spirit World for slightly over 20 years now. She was one of the kindest and most loving people I have ever known. My parents not only gave me the gift of life, but encouraged curiosity, compassion, and dedication to education. I have been very lucky in this lifetime in my journey of sharing about the beautiful gifts that our people continue to share with others. I hope that, beyond innovations and inventions, those others come to embrace the greatest gift we have given – our friendship.

Chapter 5. Sacred Circle Teachings

Call 63.iii. – Education for Reconciliation (TRC Calls to Action)

"We call upon the Council of Ministers of Education, Canada to maintain an annual commitment to Aboriginal education issues, including … building student capacity for intercultural understanding, empathy, and mutual respect."

INTRODUCTION

Growing up, and especially later in life, I have constantly heard the term *medicine wheel* being used in various settings when Indigenous peoples' issues were being discussed (e.g., education, health, politics, economics). I always wondered where the term came from and whether all Indigenous nations have a medicine wheel. Fast forward 47-plus years and I now know that the Anishinaabek have had these teachings since time immemorial. The medicine wheel, for us Anishinaabek, is one example of *bimaadziwin* (the good life). It is a living model that provides guidance to our people on how to live as honourable human beings. Therefore, education for reconciliation requires a K to 12 school system that embraces such holistic approaches to wellness, with clear plans for facilitating healthy relationships between citizens. This approach embodies Call to Action 63.iii.

As we move forward in this final chapter together, I ask you, the reader, to reflect on the following medicine-wheel facts:

- The province of Alberta has 66 percent of known medicine wheels, dispersed across the traditional lands of Treaties 6, 7, and 8 First Nations peoples and the Métis Nations (Royal Alberta Museum 2017).
- There are eight different types of medicine wheels, which have been classified by archaeologist Dr. John Brumley (Canada's Historic Places 2017).
- The term *medicine wheel* emerged from settler cultures trying to describe the Bighorn Medicine Wheel in Wyoming; medicine wheels are actually referred to as "sacred circles" in traditional Indigenous languages (Royal Alberta Museum 2017).
- The use of colours (yellow, red, black, white, blue, green) in contemporary medicine wheels did not occur until the early 1960s (see figure 5.1 for an example of a traditional medicine wheel).

Figure 5.1. Drawing of Siksika (Blackfoot) Medicine Wheel in Southern Alberta

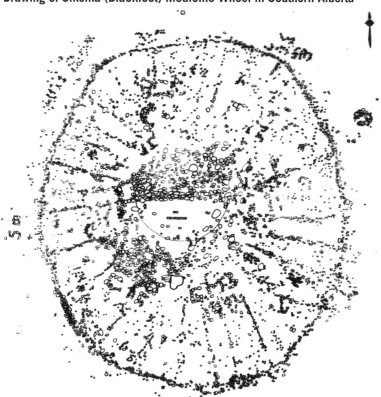

This structure is known as the "Majorville Cairn and Medicine Wheel." Archaeological studies indicate this site has been continuously used for the last 4500 years.

THE TEACHINGS OF THE SACRED CIRCLE

I have been on my own journey of learning and healing for a long time. I continue to embrace this humbling path that has given me a greater appreciation for my ancestors. The knowledge the Anishinaabek peoples possessed (and continue to possess) is rich with complexity and simplicity at the same time. The sacred circle teachings of my nation and other Indigenous nations are deeply rooted in land, culture, and language. I cannot go anywhere else in the world to have these teachings make sense to me. They come from the earth and the traditional places where we have lived for thousands of years. These teachings are the greatest indicators of how to live a good life that is balanced (see figure 5.2).

Our sacred circle is beautiful. It makes sense to me, but does it make sense to others? This is why making the sacred circle teachings contemporary for our children and youth is paramount. They can all benefit from a wellness education that embraces the whole person. They themselves, and their classmates, will be their own greatest teachers as they explore the meanings within the sacred circle. The teacher/educator becomes a facilitator and supporter in this process, and the teachings become the springboard for ongoing reflection and holistic development.

What are these teachings? The following section describes them by travelling around the sacred circle, beginning in the east and ending in the north.

Table 5.1. Sacred Circle Model and Teachings

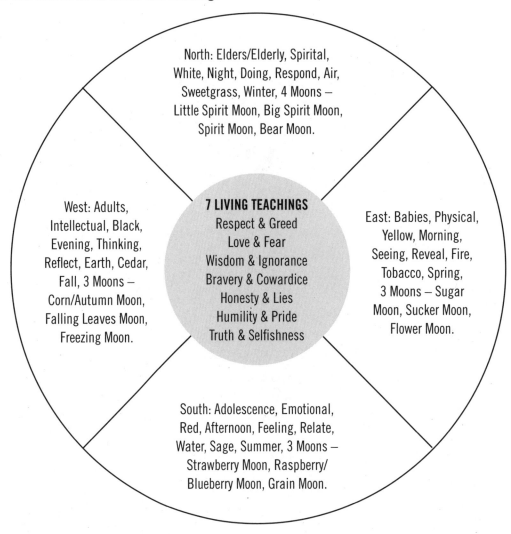

North: Elders/Elderly, Spirital,
White, Night, Doing, Respond, Air,
Sweetgrass, Winter, 4 Moons –
Little Spirit Moon, Big Spirit Moon,
Spirit Moon, Bear Moon.

West: Adults,
Intellectual, Black,
Evening, Thinking,
Reflect, Earth, Cedar,
Fall, 3 Moons –
Corn/Autumn Moon,
Falling Leaves Moon,
Freezing Moon.

7 LIVING TEACHINGS
Respect & Greed
Love & Fear
Wisdom & Ignorance
Bravery & Cowardice
Honesty & Lies
Humility & Pride
Truth & Selfishness

East: Babies, Physical,
Yellow, Morning,
Seeing, Reveal, Fire,
Tobacco, Spring,
3 Moons – Sugar
Moon, Sucker Moon,
Flower Moon.

South: Adolescence, Emotional,
Red, Afternoon, Feeling, Relate,
Water, Sage, Summer, 3 Moons –
Strawberry Moon, Raspberry/
Blueberry Moon, Grain Moon.

This sacred circle and its teachings come primarily from the Anishinaabek of the Lake Huron region.

Teachings from the East

The direction of the east is all about birth and renewal. In the life stages of a human being, the first stage is birth and infancy. The east also represents the physical, where caring for and nourishing the body is primary. The colour yellow is located here, corresponding with morning, when the sun rises in the east and embraces the Earth. The words *seeing* and *revealing* also call the east home. Seeing refers to one way of learning – by observing with all our senses. Revealing is all about our perspective. It is about both learning that we see the world as we are and being challenged to embrace other perspectives.

Fire and tobacco also go hand in hand here. Fire is the element represented by the sun and the molten heart of our Earth (magma). The teachings of fire remind us that it has the power to nurture, by warming us, or to destroy. Tobacco, as one of the four sacred medicines of the

Truth and Reconciliation in Canadian Schools

Anishinaabek, is the gift of prayer to the Creator. It is what we put down on the ground or in a sacred fire to offer our innermost thoughts.

The east is also associated with the season of spring. There are three moons in this season: Sugar Moon; Sucker Moon and Flower Moon (see figure 5.2). Each moon lasts 28 days. The ancestral knowledge of these moons comes directly from the land.

Sugar Moon represents a time when the maple tree gives our people many gifts. Syrup, taffy, and maple sugar are traditionally made during Sugar Moon, and the strength of family and relationships is emphasized. We also embrace the power of medicine and the cleansing of the physical body.

Sucker Moon holds fast to the teachings that the suckerfish gives us. This humble being travels the freshwater lakes, streams, and creeks, and cleans and purifies the lifeblood of Mother Earth. The suckerfish teaches that each of us has a role and gifts to share. It is also a time for us to pay attention to and protect our lands.

Flower Moon is the essence of diversity and beauty. During this time the earth reveals colours, textures, and shapes that are beyond our comprehension. We are constantly reminded of the magnitude of diversity in life, especially with human beings, and our sacred purpose to accept all.

Figure 5.2. Three Moons of Spring

| SUGAR MOON (28 DAYS) | SUCKER MOON (28 DAYS) | FLOWER MOON (28 DAYS) |

Approximately 84 days in the season of spring are determined by these moons.

Teachings from the South

The south is all about growth and feelings. It is a wonderful place where adolescence, the second stage of life, is located. The emotional aspect of the self is also found here and we are taught to care for ourselves and others in a good respectful way. The colour red is in this direction, representing the heat and intensity of the afternoon sun. The words *feeling* and *relating,* which are siblings in learning, also call the south home. Feeling refers to the importance of having an emotional connection to the content in our classrooms, both formal and informal. Relating takes this a step further by promoting learning that is bound to real-world experiences. The element of water is in the south and carries many teachings. One of the core insights of water is that we human beings are made up of this element. We share this physical aspect with our mother, the Earth. What flows in us also flows in her. The medicine that calls this direction home is the powerful sage, used in smudges to clear energy and provide clarity of thought.

There are three moons in summer: Strawberry Moon, Raspberry/Blueberry Moon, and Grain Moon (see figure 5.3). Strawberry Moon is directly connected to the heart. It is also a women's medicine that honours those rites of passage for young girls about to start their menstrual cycles. This moon teaches us to be kind and truthful.

Raspberry/Blueberry Moon has two significant teachings directed at boundaries and rebuilding. Raspberries teach us that we need to have healthy boundaries with others and ourselves, while blueberries teach us that we can rebuild after mass devastation.

Grain Moon is about preparation and the harvest. It challenges us to celebrate what we have and take stock of the bounty that surrounds us.

Figure 5.3. Three Moons of Summer

STRAWBERRY MOON (28 DAYS)	RASPBERRY/BLUEBERRY MOON (28 DAYS)	GRAIN MOON (28 DAYS)

Approximately 84 days in the season of summer are determined by these moons.

Teachings from the West

The west represents the third stage in human development where we continue our growth into adulthood. The west is all about change and the establishment of new routines after examining and reflecting on our personal growth. It also represents the development of our intellectual side. The colour black calls the west home, when the sun slips away and our fall evenings lengthen. The concepts of thinking and reflection also sit in this direction. Thinking is that aspect of learning where we are challenged by questions and new knowledge. Reflection extends this idea by nurturing our natural curiosity with the gifts of time and complexity.

The element of earth is located here, reminding us that the health of the Earth is reflective of our own. If she is sick, so are we. Cedar, the third sacred medicine of the Anishinaabek, is connected with the west. It can be used as a tea for curing headaches, as a salve for treating pain, as aromatherapy for peace of mind, and in many other ways.

Truth and Reconciliation in Canadian Schools

There are three moons in the season of fall: Corn/Autumn Moon, Falling Leaves Moon, and Freezing Moon (see figure 5.4). Corn/Autumn Moon represents the 13 rows of corn found on the traditional Indian corn grown by Anishinaabek and Haudenosaunee peoples. Each corn cob came in a variety of colours – a symbol that all things can thrive side by side. The diversity of kernels teaches human beings that we have the ability and skills to find ways to live and grow together respectfully.

Falling Leaves Moon is a time of celebration and warmth. Mother Earth puts on her best dress for us in colours of red, yellow, and orange. She lets us know through this action how much she loves us. This beautiful dress will return to the earth as a blanket to protect the plants and animals below.

Freezing Moon is equated with dreaming. In this 28-day space we are encouraged to think about all the possibilities that life has to offer. This moon is also when the stars seem at their brightest and closest.

Figure 5.4. Three Moons of Fall

CORN/AUTUMN MOON (28 DAYS)	FALLING LEAVES MOON (28 DAYS)	FREEZING MOON (28 DAYS)

Approximately 84 days in the season of fall are determined by these moons.

Teachings from the North

The north is all about reflection and transformation. In this direction lies the fourth stage of life, our evolution into Elders or the elderly. Our spiritual development as human beings is located here. The colour white is also synonymous with the season of winter. It represents the colour of our Grandmother Moon as she watches over us during this time. Days are short, and we spend them with her.

Doing and responding are sibling traits in the learning journey of the north. We learn through hands-on activities and by creating, inventing, and problem solving. Responding takes the concept of doing further by encouraging us to act on and expand our learning. The element of air is associated with this direction, teaching us that it has the power to change the surface of the earth. We also need air to live, an element we share with all things. The fourth sacred medicine, sweetgrass, calls the north home. It is typically braided into three parts and represents the body/mind/spirit connection that we all possess.

Chapter 5. Sacred Circle Teachings

There are four moons in winter, the largest number of all the seasons: Little Spirit Moon, Big Spirit Moon, Spirit Moon, and Bear Moon (see figure 5.5). Introspection and protection are aspects they all have in common. Little Spirit Moon is the beginning of our inner journey, a reminder to light our sacred fires and spend time with the self.

Big Spirit Moon is the next stage, reinforcing the need to purify by finding healthy ways to rid ourselves of negative energy.

Spirit Moon is the sibling of silence, the phase in which we focus our attention on listening to the teachings of our ancestors.

During Bear Moon, the final moon in winter, we are given 28 days to learn when to nurture, when to protect, and when to let go, whether of thoughts, people, or experiences.

Figure 5.5. Four Moons of Winter

LITTLE SPIRIT MOON (28 DAYS)	BIG SPIRIT MOON (28 DAYS)	SPIRIT MOON (28 DAYS)	BEAR MOON (28 DAYS)

Approximately 112 days in the season of winter are determined by these moons.

SEVEN LIVING TEACHINGS

Our children and youth not only live in a world that is changing at a faster rate than ever before, but they are also faced with unprecedented issues such as rapid climate change and the effects of ubiquitous technology on self-esteem, emotional intelligence, and relationships. They are bombarded with information daily, often every few seconds through various forms of social media. Paradoxically, although our world has become much smaller and more familiar in this digital age, a growing phenomenon of isolation exists among our children and youth (DeLoatch 2015; Xue 2013). The depth of their connections can often be superficial, measured by the number of friends, likes, or followers on social media. What can we do to help our children and youth with these challenges?

The Seven Living Teachings of the Anishinaabek sit at the heart of the sacred circle. They are often represented by seven sacred cowry shells (*megis*) on a traditional medicine wheel (Benton-Banai, 2010).

MEGIS SHELLS

Megis shells, also known as "whiteshells," are a type of cowry shell used in sacred ceremonies by Anishinaabe peoples. (Whiteshell Provincial Park in Manitoba is named after this type of shell.) Originating in the Indonesia-Pacific region, cowry shells were used worldwide as a form of currency. There is some debate about how Anishinaabe peoples traded for or found these shells, so far inland and so far north. They may have been obtained through an extensive trade network in the ancient past. Oral stories and birchbark scrolls indicate that the shells were found in the ground, or washed up on the shores of lakes or rivers.

In the Anishinaabe creation stories, Gchi-Manitou (the Creator) took the four parts of Mother Earth (earth, wind, fire, and water) and blew them in the megis shell to create the Anishinaabe peoples.

These seven teachings reflect our links to our mother, the Earth, and are described in the creation story of the Anishinaabek. These teachings are often explained as "twins," where each teaching is made up of a light energy and a dark one. I will offer concise explanations of these traditional values below.

1. **Respect and Greed**

   To honour all of Creation is to have respect (Benton-Banai 2010). Respect means demonstrating understanding and consideration for others, for the Earth, and for her children. Our own children and youth need to be able to explore real-life examples of respectful action in their families, friendships, and communities. Greed is the opposite of respect, resulting in a disregard for anything and anybody. It is the embodiment of ego in which only our needs and our often-selfish wants guide us in life. Children and youth are encouraged through this teaching to examine examples of greed in the world and how such behaviour affects people and the environment.

2. **Love and Fear**

   To know love is to know peace (ibid.). Love is an action word, or verb, in the Anishinaabemowin language. It refers to individuals behaving kindly toward each other without expectations or rewards. Our children and youth are encouraged to identify acts of kindness around them and highlight the characteristics of that individual or organization. Fear is the opposite of love, treating others (human and other-than-human) like property. To have fear is to exist in a state of non-peace and to be focused on control and ownership. It is a bottomless pit that is never satisfied. This teaching encourages children and youth to investigate examples of fear in the media (they are everywhere).

3. **Wisdom and Ignorance**

   To cherish knowledge is to know wisdom (ibid.). Wisdom encompasses our ability to have open minds, know the difference between wrong and right, and grasp the consequences, both positive and negative, of our actions. Our children and youth can be presented with various scenarios in their communities (and in pop culture) in order to critically investigate them. Developing questions is part of this process. Ignorance is the opposite of wisdom and refers to closed minds that have no regard for others and do not consider their actions or the consequences. Children and youth can be asked to provide examples of closed minds and how this attitude affects others (e.g., racism, homophobia, xenophobia).

4. **Bravery and Cowardice**

Bravery is to face the foe with integrity (ibid.). It means saying and doing the honourable and right thing in a respectful way. It also means that our stance or action may be contrary to popular belief or the status quo. Our children and youth can be challenged to investigate historical or contemporary events in which an individual or organization took a stand for a meaningful cause. Cowardice is the opposite of bravery and refers to our choice to be a bystander rather than an active participant in life. Cowardice is the action of following others, especially when they are wrong (e.g., bullying).

5. **Honesty and Lies**

Honesty in facing a situation is to be brave (ibid.). It means knowing who we are, what we stand for, and how we honour our spirit or innermost self. It also refers to our ability to acknowledge and work at changing those things or qualities that do harm. Our children and youth can be encouraged to research a family genealogy as one means of knowing who they are. Knowing what we stand for can be reinforced by investigating a person in history who displayed honesty. Lying is the opposite of honesty and is a denial of the self. Lies contribute to the illusion that we cannot change or do not have the strength to do so. Our children and youth can be encouraged to investigate issues in their communities and the world that are the result of complacency (not willing to change and living a lie).

6. **Humility and Pride**

Humility is to know oneself as a sacred part of Creation (ibid.). It also refers to our ability to accept the mystery of the universe. It means that we cannot know all things and that we give ourselves the gift of curiosity. Humility is also the celebration of interconnectedness and interrelatedness as we accept that we do not stand above others, whether human or other-than-human. Our children and youth can be asked to map out their own relationships and interdependence. An exploration of the gifts in these relationships is key. Pride is the exact opposite of humility and represents the embodiment of the ego. Pride continually seeks external reward and recognition, even when it is not deserved or earned. Children and youth can be asked to provide examples of the consequences of prideful persons (or businesses) in the world.

7. **Truth and Selfishness**

Truth is to live all these attributes (ibid.). It means to walk the talk. Truth is about recognizing that we are not perfect beings, but seek to live lives based in the teachings. We do the best we can, acknowledge when we have done wrong, and make amends. Our children and youth can be encouraged to think about people, events, and beings that are examples of truth. Selfishness is the opposite of truth and describes individuals, groups, or organizations that put their needs first and give no thought to others (including other-than-human beings). They are often hypocritical, saying one thing and doing the exact opposite (e.g., talking about kindness and then committing hurtful acts). Children and youth can be asked to investigate cases of selfishness and what activities, behaviours, and motivations preceded it.

WHY HEALTH AND PHYSICAL EDUCATION IS AN IDEAL APPROACH TO TEACHING ABOUT THE SACRED CIRCLE

Richmond and Ross (2009) highlight how environmental dispossession has adversely affected the health and identity of Indigenous peoples. It is vital for all learners to have educational programs that incorporate land-based teachings combined with outdoor activities. Accordingly, I have selected health and physical education as the focus for this chapter, using Indigenous literature as the springboard.

Table 5.2 offers ideas on how to connect health education in K to 12 classrooms with the suggested Indigenous books. These texts have been vetted by various sources and are level appropriate. The health connections (and some physical education ones) for each resource focus on a particular curricular strand that can be further explored with students. Table 5.2 offers suggestions for Indigenous games and sports that can provide the physical education aspect of a balanced wellness program. Ideally, these games and sports are played outdoors; however, teachers are encouraged to use the available space.

Table 5.2. Health and Physical Education Curriculum Connections and Resources

CURRICULUM CONNECTIONS	SUGGESTED BOOKS BY GRADE
Primary (K to 3)	
K – Self-Regulation and Well-Being – While reading the book *Little You*, ask students to identify what makes them special. After this read-aloud, encourage students (in a circle) to express and share positive messages about each other.	**K** – *Little You* by Richard Van Camp (2013)
1 – Personal Safety and Injury Prevention – After reading *Mama, Do You Love Me?*, ask students to identify what caring behaviours are and the feelings that go with them. Extend this discussion by talking about exploitative behaviours and what to do about them.	**1** – *Mama, Do You Love Me?* by Barbara M. Joosse (1991)
2 – Interpersonal Skills – Before reading *Thanks to the Animals*, have students identify people they know and the reasons they are thankful for them. After reading the book, encourage students to use positive language toward each other.	**2** – *Thanks to the Animals* by Allen Sockabasin (2014)
3 – Human Development and Sexual Health – While reading *Taan's Moons: A Haida Moon Story*, ask students to identify the factors that affected the bears' development and growth during this story. Extend this activity by having them list the factors that affect their own overall health.	**3** – *Taan's Moons: A Haida Moon Story* by Alison Gear (2014)

CURRICULUM CONNECTIONS	SUGGESTED BOOKS BY GRADE

Junior (4 to 6)

4 – Personal Skills – Read *Where Only Elders Go – Moon Lake Loon Lake*. Review the key themes in this story (the life cycle of a human being, importance of relationships, death and loss). Ask students to identify feelings that are especially associated with death and loss and the strategies for healthy coping. **5 – Movement Strategies** – Before you read *The Drum Calls Softly*, ask students to think about the features of the round dance described in this book. After reading, extend these ideas by making connections to their current physical activities. **6 – Critical and Creative Thinking** – While reading *A Coyote Solstice Tale*, ask students to identify the various stereotypes and assumptions being made. Extend this conversation by listing social activities that friends can engage in without the key focus being consumerism, as presented in the book.	**4** – *Where Only Elders Go – Moon Lake Loon Lake* by Jan Bourdeau Waboose (2003) **5** – *The Drum Calls Softly* by David Bouchard and Shelley Willier (2008) **6** – *A Coyote Solstice Tale* by Thomas King (2009)

Intermediate (7 and 8)

7 – Active Participation – While reading the *Adventures of Rabbit and Bear Paws: Tall Tale*, ask students to keep a list of the indoor and outdoor activities in the story. Discuss the unique aspects of these activities and how they compare and differ to their current range of physical activities. **8 – Personal Safety and Injury Prevention** – While reading *The Way: A Novel*, have students identify the violent behaviours in this book. Extend this discussion by analyzing the impact of this violence on the person, the perpetrator, and the bystanders, and the key role of helpers (e.g., Uncle John).	**7** – *Adventures of Rabbit and Bear Paws: Tall Tale* by Chad Solomon and Christopher Meyer (2010) **8** – *The Way: A Novel* by Joseph Bruchac (2007)

Secondary (9 to 12)

9 – Healthy Active Living Education, Healthy Eating – Use the *Anishinaabe Almanac: Living Through the Seasons* to develop a holistic model of health with students (active living; healthy eating; mental, emotional, and spiritual health). Extend this activity with a conversation on the benefits of adopting a holistic approach. **10 – Healthy Active Living Education, Personal Safety, and Injury Prevention** – While reading *Fire Starters*, have students highlight the situations involving conflict in the story (being blamed for something you did not do, community attitudes/values, racism). Extend this conversation by discussing similar situations and how conflict-resolution skills might have been helpful.	**9** – *Anishinaabe Almanac: Living Through the Seasons* by Edward Benton-Banai (2008) **10** – *Fire Starters* by Jen Storm (2016)

Truth and Reconciliation in Canadian Schools

CURRICULUM CONNECTIONS	SUGGESTED BOOKS BY GRADE
11 – Health for Life, Personal Safety, and Injury Prevention – Read *Three Feathers: A Graphic Novel* and have students describe the behaviours of the main characters (Flinch, Bryce, Rupert) and the remedy applied by the community. Extend this activity by having a conversation about the nine-month reconciliation program described in the book and how it can reduce the risk of injury and death. **12 – Recreation and Healthy Active Living Leadership, Personal Safety, and Injury Prevention** – Read the graphic novel *Will I See?* Extend this reading by exploring the phenomena and occurrence of violence against Indigenous women and the actions that need to be taken to protect/honour their lives. Discuss the implications of these issues in their community (e.g., the incidence of violence and the programs in place).	**11** – *Three Feathers: A Graphic Novel* by Richard Van Camp (2014) **12** – *Will I See?* by David Alexander Robertson and Iskwé (2016)

The curriculum connections in this table come from modified versions of specific expectations in the Ontario curriculum (elementary and secondary health/physical education courses). These strands engage students with that particular book in a variety of ways.

Table 5.3. Integrating Indigenous Games into Schools

GRADE	SUGGESTED GAMES AND RESOURCES
K	Bone and Toggle Game (Eastern Woodland) http://www.virtualmuseum.ca/edu/ViewLoitLo.do?method=preview&lang=EN&id=11721
1	Dice or Deer Button Game (Eastern Woodland) http://www.virtualmuseum.ca/edu/ViewLoitLo.do?method=preview&lang=EN&id=11721
2	Snowsnake (Eastern Woodland) http://www.virtualmuseum.ca/edu/ViewLoitLo.do?method=preview&lang=EN&id=11721
3	Bone and Stick Game (Inuit) http://icor.ottawainuitchildrens.com/node/23
4	One Foot High Kick (Inuit) http://icor.ottawainuitchildrens.com/node/39
5	Back Push (Inuit) http://icor.ottawainuitchildrens.com/node/39
6	Line Tag (Plains) http://opi.mt.gov/PDF/IndianEd/Search/Health%20Enhancement/G4%20Line%20Tag.pdf
7	Double Ball (Plains) http://www.spsd.sk.ca/Schools/brightwater/teacher/midteachers/resources/Documents/First%20Nations%20Double%20Ball%20Game%20Instructions.pdf

GRADE	SUGGESTED GAMES AND RESOURCES
8	Hoop and Arrow (Plains)
	http://www.manataka.org/page185.html
9	Canoeing (West and East Coast)
	https://www.sfu.ca/brc/art_architecture/canoes.html
10	La Plotte (Métis)
	http://blog.scs.sk.ca/fnmieteam/physical_fnmie_integration_guide
	_grade%206%20to%208.pdf
11	The Pole Push (West Coast and Subarctic)
	https://jmautihealthphysicaleducation.wikispaces.com/Aboriginal+Games+%26+Activities
12	Lacrosse (Haudenosaunee)
	https://archaeologymuseum.ca/traditional-games-workshop/

These traditional Indigenous games are only a select few out of hundreds that were — and are — played in Canada. Each website listed provides instructions or information for the game mentioned.

CONCLUSION

The sacred circle. Evolving. Continuous. Whole. These are the words that describe this model for living a good and honourable life. I have come to know what many refer to as the medicine wheel in a deeply personal way. These Anishinaabek teachings have brought perspective into my own life. I often sit and reflect on my growth as a human being and as a teacher, trying to think of ways I can be more of a helper in this educational and life journey. I do the best that I can to fulfill my role and respect my dodem (clan).

The greatest lesson that the sacred circle has given me is one of gratitude. The word *meegwetch*, from my language of Anishinaabemowin, translates into the English word "thanks," but means so much more than that. It embodies the necessity for living a life that values Creation and all that the Creator has provided. Meegwetch means that I walk forward, looking back to the teachings of my ancestors, and preparing this world for the next seven generations. This challenge is one I have accepted, and I hope that you, the reader, will accept it, as well.

PART 2

Truth and Reconciliation
Lesson Plans by Grade

Introduction to Part 2: Lesson Format and Scope/Sequence

The lessons that follow take a holistic approach modelled on Indigenous pedagogy and student success. To ensure balanced student learning, each lesson focuses on all four aspects of the Anishinaabe sacred circle: spiritual, physical, emotional, and intellectual. The background information provides the knowledge that educators need to move forward with each lesson, including key terms. Teachers should always review the background information first.

1. **Spiritual**

   The Spiritual is represented by an Indigenous concept, a specific teaching, a historical fact, or a traditional use related to the topic. The concept or other element is always paired with an image that exemplifies it or is connected to it. If you choose, you can enlarge and display the image, and/or share the chosen teaching or fact with the class before the lesson. It may help establish a more intimate connection to the material for you and your students.

2. **Physical**

   The Physical includes the time, materials, resources, considerations, and suggested adaptations required to implement the lesson with the whole class (or enhance it). Each of these lessons is an introductory springboard to the topic and needs to be covered first if students are not familiar with the content. If your students are familiar with the topic, then you can focus the lesson further by using the Suggested Adaptations by Subject.

3. **Emotional**

   The Emotional includes both the strategies required for student engagement and the learning goal and step-by-step plans needed to carry out the lesson. It is vital for teachers to review this section thoroughly to map out or adjust the lesson plan. The learning goal is supported through the interactive classroom activities, beginning with a Minds-On activity for focusing the learning and/or creating curiosity about the topic. The lesson ends with a Consolidation activity that uses questions to connect the learning to students' experiences.

4. **Intellectual**

   The Intellectual is represented by the assessment strategies, suggested extensions, and reproducible masters (RM) needed to carry out and/or further develop the lesson with the class. Each reproducible is an organizer that will be used in the lesson.

SCOPE/SEQUENCE OF LESSONS

The Calls to Action of the Truth and Reconciliation Commission of Canada Report (TRC) asked that a national K to 12 curriculum on residential schools, treaties, teachings, empathy, and understanding be created and implemented. Figure 6.1 embraces that challenge and proposes themes by grade-specific divisions that build on each other. **Learning Together** in K to 3 focuses on exploring Mother Earth knowledge and the perspectives of First Nation, Métis, and Inuit peoples. **Building Community** in Grades 4 to 6 helps develop relationships and compassion among students while investigating Indigenous contributions, treaties, and residential schools. **Facilitating Change** in Grades 7 to 8 honours adolescent questioning of authority and embarks on activities related to truth-telling and celebrations. **Transforming Lives** in Grades 9 to 12 builds on the individuality of youth and on social-justice movements while incorporating meaningful activities related to Indigenous child protection and the plight of Indigenous women.

Figure 6.1. Themes for Lesson Plans Organized by Divisions

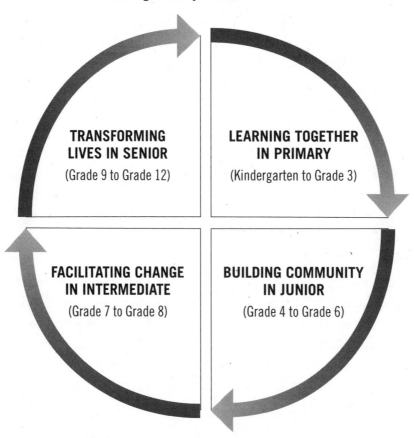

This model is reflective of scope and sequence for learning about Indigenous peoples in an age-appropriate manner. However, flexibility in topics may be necessary depending on the dynamics of your school and area. This model builds on the Calls to Action on education for reconciliation in the TRC Report and select subjects in the Ontario curriculum.

Kindergarten Lesson Plan — Mother Earth

BACKGROUND INFORMATION FOR TEACHERS

Every Indigenous nation has its own word for Mother Earth in its original language. The teachings of Mother Earth and the gifts she gives us also vary among First Nation, Métis, and Inuit peoples. However, caring for the Earth and being good stewards is one of the key principles that all Indigenous nations share. Mother Earth is personified and everything is seen as alive. Being outside and learning about the outdoors is a key teaching strategy with all students.

KEY TERMS

Mother Earth: a name that Indigenous peoples often use to describe the world we live in.

garden: a piece of ground where various plants (vegetables, fruit, herbs) are grown.

SPIRITUAL

Mother Earth is an original and ancient being. Her children (plants and animals) live in harmony. The two-leggeds (humans) are entrusted with taking care of her and her children. All of life is therefore interconnected. The health of Mother Earth is a mirror for our own well-being.

PHYSICAL

Time: 100 minutes

Materials/Resources

- *Lessons from Mother Earth* by Elaine McLeod (2010)
- materials for students to create their own gardens (real or imagined)
- Mother Earth Collage (RM K.1)
- magazines and flyers
- glue
- crayons
- chart paper
- markers

Considerations

- Find out the local Indigenous name (with the meaning) for Mother Earth. Share with students.
- Do not use past tense when discussing the teachings of Indigenous peoples about stewardship of the Earth.

Suggested Adaptations by Frame

- **Belonging and Contributing** – Talk with your students about their own families' teachings and experiences with the Earth. Communicate these ideas through various art forms (e.g., drama, dance, music, visual arts).
- **Self-Regulation and Well-Being** – Help your students to find opportunities outdoors to develop empathy for the plant and animal beings on the Earth (e.g., keep the playground clean, make bird feeders).
- **Demonstrating Literacy and Mathematics Behaviours** – Use new vocabulary from the book (e.g., Mother Earth, garden) and integrate mathematics terms (bigger/smaller, closer/farther) as the learning moment comes up.
- **Problem Solving and Innovating** – Select materials for students to create their own gardens (real or imagined). Talk about the importance of these materials to the garden (e.g., water, soil, rocks).

EMOTIONAL

Learning Goal

To gain a deeper appreciation of Mother Earth and all the gifts she provides.

Step by Step

Minds-On

1. Take your students outside. Ask them what they see and hear. Give them prompts like "Can you see something that is living and is green?" "Does the wind make a sound?" Always connect the questions and prompts to nature, weather, and animals.

2. Take your students back to the classroom. At your circle or carpet area, ask students to share what they saw and heard while outside.

3. Show them the cover of the book *Lessons from Mother Earth*. Tell them they are going to be hearing a story about a little girl, her grandma, and all the things the girl sees, hears, tastes, smells, and feels while working in the garden and out on the land.

During

1. Read the story *Lessons from Mother Earth*. Pause in the sections of the story that connect to students' experiences outdoors today (e.g., plants, weather, animals). Have your students identify the similarities and differences between their own landscapes and those in the book.

2. Conclude your Read-Aloud by having students stand up. Remind them to stay on their spots and be safe. Guide them in using their bodies to demonstrate various aspects of nature from the story (e.g., reach high to the sky like the trees around Grandma's house; move your arms softly like the gentle wind at Grandma's house; on the spot, pretend you are walking in Grandma's garden).

3. Have students sit back down at their spots in the circle or carpet area. Show them a larger version of the Mother Earth collage (RM K.1) that you have recreated on chart paper. Take a magazine or flyer and gently tear out an image of a plant, animal, or element (air, water, fire, earth). Glue a couple of selected images on the Mother Earth collage. Let students know that these are the things you love about Mother Earth. Point to each image and say its name (e.g., blueberries, trees, birds).

4. Send students back to their tables or desks, and provide copies of the Mother Earth collage (RM K.1) so they can complete the same activity. This is their own personal Mother Earth collage.

5. Once students have completed their collages, ask them to focus on nature's gifts at your classroom learning centres (e.g., at the paint centre, they can create scenes from nature; at the building centre, they can recreate Grandma's garden; at the book centre, they can select a book about Mother Earth).

Consolidation

- Bring students back together at the circle or carpet area and have them pretend they are walking with Grandma in the woods.

- Review the Key Terms (*Mother Earth* and *garden*) and place on your word wall, along with definitions.

- Wrap up students' learning by asking these questions:
  - What are some of your favourite things that Mother Earth gives to us?
  - How does Mother Earth help us?
  - Why is it important for us to take care of Mother Earth?

INTELLECTUAL

Assessment

For – Establishing prior knowledge of Mother Earth and her attributes using a seeing/hearing activity outdoors.

As – Students' completion of Mother Earth Collage captures all the things they love about the Earth.

Of – Responses to questions on Mother Earth (what they love, how she helps us, why she is important).

EXTENSIONS

- Invite a local Indigenous Elder or Métis Senator to the classroom to talk about Mother Earth.
- Go on a medicine walk with a local Indigenous Elder, Métis Senator, or cultural resource person.

MOTHER EARTH COLLAGE

Name: _____

These are the things I love about Mother Earth.	Glue your images here.

Grade One Lesson Plan — First Nations

BACKGROUND INFORMATION FOR TEACHERS

There are more than 630 First Nation communities in this country, representing over 50 diverse nations and languages. It is important to know that every First Nation community has its own teachings and respected Elders. Each First Nation is also on its own journey of healing and reclaiming of culture. This is why it is important to establish a relationship with a local First Nation. Acknowledging the First Nation territory where the school is located is a strong step toward building that connection. Integrating local First Nation knowledge is a key teaching strategy with all students.

KEY TERMS

First Nations: a term used to describe the original peoples of Canada who have lived here for thousands of years.

teachings: ideas, principles, and values that are shared by Elders and other respected persons with their families, communities, and others as appropriate.

SPIRITUAL

First Nations are diverse in their values, languages, and ceremonies. Their Elders are respected knowledge keepers who hold ancestral histories. The teachings of First Nations are rooted in the sacred; all things are living. We are spiritual beings and are to treat each other with kindness and truth.

PHYSICAL

Time: 100 minutes

Truth and Reconciliation in Canadian Schools

Materials/Resources

- First Nations music
- *A Big Mistake?* by Richelle Lovegrove (2014)
- Teachings We Are Learning (RM 1.1)
- chart paper
- markers
- crayons

Considerations

- Find a local First Nation name and description for a grandmother. Share this word and the significance of this individual with students.
- Do not oversimplify the role that Elders have within their families and communities. Their teachings are a vast library of knowledge.

Suggested Adaptations by Subject

The Arts

Integrate a variety of First Nations music throughout this lesson. Connect the lyrics and mood of the music to a sharing of teachings (e.g., drum songs are examples of the heartbeat of Mother Earth and teach us to take care of her).

Social Studies

Identify significant events that occur in the lives of your students (e.g., new sibling, a trip, a move, new grade and class) and what this has taught them. Connect this learning to events and teachings in the story (e.g., Summer giving the necklace away).

Health and Physical Education

Focus on examples of caring behaviours in your students' lives and in the story. Investigate the feelings they have with these types of interactions (e.g., positive words make me feel happy; sharing with others makes me feel like I'm part of a family).

Science and Technology

Describe ways to show respect for each other and the Earth. Link these examples to how these activities create a healthy environment for all (e.g., planting trees and taking care of them creates good healthy air for us).

Mathematics

Use select math language (positional terms) to describe locations of people, places, and things in the story and in real life (e.g., Summer is sitting beside her cat, Kokum is sitting inside at the table; I am standing in front of my desk, I am sitting near the window).

EMOTIONAL

Learning Goal

To explore teachings from a First Nation source and from personal experiences.

Step by Step

Minds-On

1. Gather students at your Read-Aloud area (circle or carpet). Show them the cover of the book, *A Big Mistake?* Ask them to think about the title and share with an elbow partner what they think the book is about.

2. On chart paper, create a T-Chart. At the top of the first column write "What We Think," and in the second column write "What We Know."

3. In the first column, record some of the predictions that students make about the contents of the book. Review these predictions. Set a reading goal with students to focus on what the book is about (e.g., characters, setting, messages).

During

1. Read the story *A Big Mistake?* Discuss the content of the story with your students. Record their insights in the second column of your T-Chart. Ask them to think about the differences and similarities between the two columns. Were their predictions accurate?

2. Review the Key Terms (*First Nations* and *teachings*, plus definitions) with students. Tell them this story comes from First Nations people, specifically the Ojibwe. This book provides a sharing opportunity for teachings about friendship and being thankful.

3. Ask your students to stand up on their spots. Remind them to be safe and respect others' space. Let them know you are doing an activity called "Giving Thanks." Use these prompts (with body movement): "Clap your hands if you're thankful for your friends. Stomp your feet if you're thankful for recess. Rub your stomach if you're thankful for good food. Give a thumbs up if you're thankful for this beautiful day. Smile at a friend or your teacher if you're thankful when someone shares with you."

4. Have your students sit back down at their spots. Ask them to give examples of sharing. Build upon these examples by linking the sharing of teachings as also important. Highlight the teachings of Kokum from the book, *A Big Mistake?* Ask students to share other examples of teachings they have learned from their families and communities.

5. On chart paper, recreate a larger version of Teachings We Are Learning (RM 1.1). In the first column, record examples of teachings that students have learned from the story. In the second column, record examples of teachings they have learned from their families and communities.

Truth and Reconciliation in Canadian Schools

6. Tell students they will be creating their own Teachings We Are Learning. Their task is to draw two pictures: (1) an example from the story of a teaching being shared or learned, and (2) an example from their own families or communities of a teaching being shared or learned.

7. Ask students to return to their desks or tables, and have them complete the activity.

8. After students have finished the activity, ask them to focus on teachings about friendship, sharing, and being thankful at the various classroom learning centres (e.g., at the art centre they can create scenes of things they are thankful for, at the book centre they can choose a book about friendship, at the music centre they can create a shared musical piece with a partner or triad).

Consolidation

- Bring students back together at your Read-Aloud area by having them pretend they are joining Summer and Kokum (from the story) for supper, as shown in the book.
- Wrap up their learning by asking these questions:
  - What is your favourite part of the story in *A Big Mistake?*
  - How does Kokum help Summer? And us?
  - Why is it important for us to listen to teachings?

INTELLECTUAL

Assessment

For – Making predictions about the content of the book as a means to establish prior knowledge.

As – Completion of visual organizer that documents student understanding of teachings from the book and from his/her life.

Of – Responses to questions that highlight the key concepts of teachings and sharing.

EXTENSIONS

- Implement a Grandparent's Chair in your classroom for a day. Have a respected Elder spend the day in your class. His/her role and involvement is determined by your students throughout that day.
- Have a First Nations book fair at your library. This will allow you and your students to experience more First Nations literature that is authentic and meaningful.

TEACHINGS WE ARE LEARNING

Name: _____

Teachings from the Book	Teachings from My Home
Draw your picture below.	Draw your picture below.

Grade Two Lesson Plan — Métis

BACKGROUND INFORMATION FOR TEACHERS

Métis peoples are diverse in their histories and teachings. Some Métis trace their roots back to the Red River, Manitoba, and to Louis Riel. Many Métis also trace their lineage back to varied Indigenous and European nations. The identity of the Métis is unique, and they possess an emerging place in Canadian/Indigenous society. Their original Métis language is called "Michif," a complex blend of French, Cree, and Ojibwe. The Elders of this nation are called "Métis Senators." They hold the teachings and stories of their peoples.

KEY TERMS

Métis: peoples from mixed Indigenous and European ancestry who are recognized under the Constitution of Canada.

generosity: the act of being kind and understanding by willingly giving time, material goods, and/or money.

SPIRITUAL

Métis values are expressed in their relationships with the land and with each other. The teachings of kindness, strength, tolerance, honesty, courage, love, respect, patience, balance, sharing, and caring are embedded in these connections. The stories and teachings embody these principles.

PHYSICAL

Time: 100 minutes

Materials/Resources

- *The Giving Tree: A Retelling of a Traditional Métis Story* by Leah Dorion (2009)
- chart paper
- markers
- My Giving Tree (RM 2.1)
- crayons

Considerations

- Find local Métis teachings about generosity and the importance of nature. Share with students.
- Do not assume that all Métis peoples have the same histories, teachings, and values.

Suggested Adaptations by Subject

The Arts

Use dance (movement, space) to illustrate parts of the story, using a variety of pathways, directions, and shapes in nature (e.g., curvy, zigzag, forward, sideways, big trees, small trees). Vary the groupings in these dance creations (e.g., partner, triad, quad, whole class).

Social Studies

Integrate the celebrations and achievements of Métis peoples, like the reverence for nature through the giving tree (in the book), the success of the fur trade (because of Métis women), and the creation of beautiful beaded clothing (on trousers, jackets, and adornments for horses). Connect these celebrations and achievements to the unique traditions that your students bring to the classroom. Compare similarities and differences in a respectful manner (e.g., the birth of a baby has a special celebration among Métis; what are the customs among your students?).

Health and Physical Education

Discuss the benefits of physical activity for Métis peoples in the story and why it was essential (e.g., travelling to the giving tree, trade reasons, Red River carts). Have students identify their own reasons for being active and its importance for good health.

Science and Technology

Focus on the ways people and things such as Métis travellers, Red River carts, and trees move throughout the story (e.g., turning, spinning, vibrating, swinging, rolling). Recreate these movements with your students by using the appropriate scientific language (e.g., push, pull, wheel, inclined plane).

Mathematics

Investigate the relationships of time in the story (days, weeks, months, years) with students. Connect these time relationships to students' own lives with examples (e.g., their ages, special occasions, start of the school year, end of the school year).

EMOTIONAL

Learning Goal

To discover the concept of generosity among Métis peoples and your students.

Step by Step

Minds-On

1. Take your students to a location in the playground where they can observe trees.
2. Use these focus questions: What colours is/are the tree/trees? How are they shaped? Does anyone live in these trees? Why are they important?
3. Form a circle with your students. Ask them to show what one of the trees looks like, using their bodies. You may have to model an example for them first. Repeat this activity by having them recreate a tree shape with a partner, in triads, and in quads.
4. Ask students what they love the most about trees. Take them back inside the classroom.

During

1. Gather your students at your Read-Aloud area. Review the Key Terms (*Métis* and *generosity*) with them. Place these words on your word wall.
2. Show students the cover of the book *The Giving Tree*. Let them know they are going to hear a beautiful story about Métis peoples and their relationship with a tree.
3. Read the story. Pause at the sections where Métis peoples leave gifts in the tree (e.g., food, utensils). Ask students why Métis peoples would leave items in the tree. Take this a step further and ask them what they would leave in the tree for others.
4. Finish reading the story. With an elbow partner, have students share the items they would leave in the tree.
5. Ask students to stand up on their spots. Remind them to be safe while doing this activity. Guide them in this bodily-kinesthetic teaching strategy in which they pretend to be a tree in the seasons. Begin with the season you are in and work around the year (e.g., "Show me what a tree looks like in spring with the rain falling on it"; "Show me what a tree looks like in the fall when its leaves are tumbling to the ground.").
6. Complete this activity, and have students sit at their spots. On chart paper, recreate a larger version of My Giving Tree (RM 2.1). Using words and images, record the things that you and your students would put in your giving tree. Record these words and images

around or on the tree. Review these items. Let students know they will be completing their own giving trees at their desks.

7. Give each student a copy of RM 2.1, and ask students to work on their own giving trees.

At your classroom learning centres, ask students to focus on the importance of giving and the importance of trees (e.g., at the art centre they can create scenes of forests and the animals in them, at the book centre they can choose a book about giving, at the science centre they can use magnifying glasses to examine pictures of various trees).

Consolidation

- Bring students back together at your Read-Aloud area, and have them pretend they are Métis travellers from the story driving their Red River carts.

- Wrap up their learning by asking these questions:
  - What is your favourite part of the story in *The Giving Tree*?
  - How do the Métis travellers help each other?
  - Why is it important for us to listen to these teachings?

INTELLECTUAL

Assessment

For – Tree activity outdoors that establishes curiosity and students' prior knowledge.

As – Discussion of items students would place in the giving tree, and completion of visual organizer.

Of – Responses to questions that highlight the importance of generosity and reciprocity.

EXTENSIONS

- Invite a Métis Senator to the classroom to share the teachings of the Métis nation.
- Plant tree seedlings with your class as part of Earth Day or Earth Week.

MY GIVING TREE

Name: _____

Write or draw the things you would put in your giving tree.

Grade Three Lesson Plan — Inuit

BACKGROUND INFORMATION FOR TEACHERS

The Inuit peoples are one of the most resilient Indigenous Nations, learning to live in harmony with the coldest environments in Canada. They are renowned for their many contributions in the arts, human rights, and protection of the globe (northern lands and animals). Inuk (referring to one person) is the singular form of Inuit. As of 2016 the median age for Inuit peoples is 23 years. Approximately 60 percent of Inuit are able to have a conversation in their original language.

KEY TERMS

Inuit: the name of the original Indigenous peoples living in northern Canada (Nunavut, Northwest Territories, northern Quebec, and northern Labrador) whose mother language is Inuktitut.

tundra: a large flat area of land in the northern regions of the world with no trees (or very small trees), but plentiful with lichens and mosses. The ground below the top layer of soil is always frozen. Despite the cold, many animals live on the tundra, including insects, migrating birds, and foxes.

SPIRITUAL

The Inuit believe that all things have spirits and are to be treated as sacred. They have a deep bond with their lands and animals. Hunting and fishing are part of daily life. Every part of the animals is used, and prayers before and after hunting are offered to thank this relation. A loving understanding of the interconnectedness of all things is what makes the Inuit unique.

PHYSICAL

Time: 100 minutes

Materials/Resources

- various images of the Arctic (e.g., northern lights, icescapes, Arctic Ocean, Arctic foxes, polar bears)
- various images of Inuit art
- various resources about Arctic plants, Inuit way of life, Inuit games
- *Wild Eggs: A Tale of Arctic Egg Hunting* by Suzie Napayok (2015)
- chart paper
- markers
- Out on the Land (RM 3.1)
- crayons

Considerations

- Contact an Inuit organization and ask about recommended resources for exploring Inuit culture further. Share these resources with students.
- Do not use the term *Eskimo*. Try to use names that are identified by the Inuit themselves.

Suggested Adaptations by Subject

The Arts

Integrate Inuit art into this lesson. Focus on how these various two- and three-dimensional works of art have been inspired by nature.

Social Studies

Investigate Inuit ways of life during the early 19th century with a specific focus on foods, values, and interrelationships in families. Have students make connections between these findings and their own communities.

Health and Physical Education

Include various Inuit games and sports as part of this lesson (e.g., one-foot-high kick, blanket toss). Concentrate on the skills and movements that make these activities unique (e.g., static positions, different levels like high/medium/low, with or without equipment).

Science and Technology

Create opportunities for students to research the plants of the Arctic and to learn how the plants respond to changes in the environment. Offer a variety of resources as part of these investigations (e.g., websites, encyclopedias, DVDs, other nonfiction sources).

Mathematics

Explore symmetry in a variety of Inuit art (e.g., sculptures, paintings, designs in clothing). Have students complete an aspect of Inuit art by drawing in a missing portion.

EMOTIONAL

Learning Goal

To relate to the teachings of the Inuit through relationships and connections to land.

Step by Step

Minds-On

1. Set up your images of the Arctic around the classroom.
2. Tell students they are going on a gallery walk in the classroom. Let them know that this is your Arctic walk.
3. Have students walk around the room looking at the images. Remind them to be safe and to respect each other's space.
4. Ask them to think about what their favourite image is, and why.
5. Guide them to your Read-Aloud area. Have a brief discussion about what they loved in this gallery walk and why they chose that image.

During

1. Show them the cover of the book *Wild Eggs: A Tale of Arctic Egg Hunting*. Ask them to predict what the story is about.
2. Share the Key Terms (*Inuit* and *tundra*) with students. Let them know that these two words are hints about the content of the book.
3. Read the story and pause at the sections where Akuluk (the main character) and her grandfather discover new things on the land (e.g., animals, different types of eggs). Ask students to show you (with their hands) the shape or movement of that object.
4. After you finish reading the story, have students share with you the things that Akuluk discovered with her grandfather on the land. Record these objects on the chart paper. Review these objects with the class.
5. Let students know they are going to do a similar activity. Say: "We're going to get dressed and go out to the playground. We're going to walk around and see what things are out on the land at this place." Take your students outside for a brief period.
6. Bring students back to the Read-Aloud area. On chart paper, make a list of all the things they saw out on the land (the playground). Review the list.

7. Ask students to return to their desks and tables. Give each student a copy of Out On the Land (RM 3.1). Let them know they are to complete their own version. Ask them to focus on things they saw that are not on the big list, and what they would like to see in the playground (e.g., more trees, a splash park).

8. Once students have completed their activity, ask them to focus on nature themes at your classroom learning centres (e.g., at the art centre they can create scenes of special places in nature, at the book centre they can select a book about weather and the seasons, at the science centre they can review materials about animals and their habitats).

Consolidation

- Bring your students back together at your Read-Aloud area, and have them pretend they are Akuluk from the story, walking on the tundra.
- Wrap up their learning by asking these questions:
  - What is your favourite part of the story in *Wild Eggs: A Tale of Arctic Egg Hunting?*
  - How does Akuluk learn from her grandfather?
  - Why is it important for us to spend time with our trusted Elders?

INTELLECTUAL

Assessment

For – Gallery walk of Arctic images and discussion establishes prior knowledge.

As – Focused walk in the playground and completion of Out On the Land (RM 3.1).

Of – Responses to questions that centre around learning from our Elders.

EXTENSIONS

- Complete a virtual tour of the Arctic using available media and technology.
- Coordinate a pen pal activity with a school in the Arctic via social media.

OUT ON THE LAND

Name: _____

This is what we found out on the land.

Grade Four Lesson Plan — Contributions

BACKGROUND INFORMATION FOR TEACHERS

Every Indigenous nation has stories and teachings about the sky. Indigenous peoples are strongly connected to sky phenomena and refer to the sun, moon, and constellations as family members (e.g., Grandmother Moon, Sky Woman, The Great Bear). Often the personal names of Indigenous peoples reflected the seasonal behaviours of the sky (e.g., Thunder Being, Rain). The stars were also used as a means of determining direction on land and on water. Understanding and describing the constellations is only one of the many contributions that Indigenous peoples have made.

KEY TERMS

constellation: a group of stars that appear to form a picture in the sky and are typically named after animals, objects, or myths.

contribution: something (e.g., action, material) that we give to help a cause, community, group, or person.

SPIRITUAL

Sky stories are part of the highly complex spirituality of Indigenous peoples. Each nation has its own unique and distinctive sky stories. For example, the Anishinaabe speak of Kiwetinanang, the Guardian of the North (pictured to the right). He and his companion, the wolf, bring winter and old age to the cycle of life. (See "Teachings from the North" in Chapter 5, Sacred Circle Teachings, for more information.)

PHYSICAL

Time: 100 minutes

Materials/Resources

- images of the sky (e.g., day, night, northern lights, sunrise, sunset, storms)
- resources about stars, sky, and space, including those with Indigenous perspectives
- connecting cubes
- *Warren Whistles at the Sky* by David A. Robertson (2016)
- Contributions Everywhere (RM 4.1)
- chart paper
- markers
- Keoke and Porterfield's *Encyclopedia of American Indian Contributions to the World* by E. D. Keoke and K. M. Porterfield (2003)
- resources about contributing (e.g., books, Internet)
- pencil crayons
- pastels
- paper

Considerations

- Find local Indigenous names (with their meanings) for the sky, stars, sun, or moon. Share with students.
- Do not present Indigenous stories and knowledge of the constellations as untrue or as fantasy.

Suggested Adaptations by Subject

The Arts

Create two to three physical step-dance sequences that are based on sky phenomena and nature (e.g., in a three-step sequence, have students become a cloud, then rain falling to the ground, then evaporating as the sun comes out).

Social Studies

Compare the beliefs of two Indigenous nations about the sky and the environment. Compare these beliefs and practices in older times and today (e.g., How does the understanding of the sky affect current practices? Do the teachings about the sky affect the picking of medicines or growing of plants?).

Truth and Reconciliation in Canadian Schools

Health and Physical Education

Mirror the movement and journeys of various sky and space phenomena by using different locomotor movements, speeds, levels, pathways, and directions (e.g., create an obstacle course that models the journey of an asteroid through space).

Science and Technology

Investigate the light properties of the stars and the moon compared with those of human-made objects (e.g., candles, safety reflectors). Describe the differences between those that emit their own light and those that reflect it.

Mathematics

Use connecting cubes to recreate pictures of stars and constellations. Scaffold these activities from simple to complex sky phenomena. Encourage students to work together in solving these problems.

EMOTIONAL

Learning Goal

To explore the contributions of Indigenous peoples and those of students' worlds.

Step by Step

Minds-On

1. Show students a variety of images of the sky. Place a few of these images around the room. Ask students to go and stand by the image they love most. Remind them to do so safely and respectfully. Ask them to share with their elbow partner why they chose that image of the sky. Have a few of your students share their reasons for choosing that image with the class.

2. Have students return to their desks. Give them pastels and paper. Explain that they are each going to create a personal sky picture. Remind them they have many images around the room to help them with design.

3. Once students have completed their sky pictures, place the pictures around the room. Ask students to share with an elbow partner what they love about each other's sky picture.

During

1. Review the Key Terms (*constellation* and *contribution*) with the class. Let students know we all make contributions every day. Good contributions can make us feel good about ourselves and others, like creating a beautiful sky picture for the class and sharing it with others.

2. Show students the cover of the book *Warren Whistles at the Sky* and have them predict the theme. What does the cover tell us about the story?

3. Set a reading goal with students to try and remember at least one constellation (or legend) from the story.

4. After you finish reading, ask your students to stand up if they remember at least one constellation or legend. Typically the whole class will be standing. If a couple of students are still seated, ask them to stand up if they remember the name of the main character (Warren). Now the whole class will be standing. Have your students find a space in the room where they are not touching anyone. Let them know they will be doing a bodily-kinesthetic activity called "Gifts from the Sky."

5. Call out the constellations and sky phenomena in the story by name (e.g., northern lights, the Big Dipper). Ask students to use their bodies to show you what each phenomenon looks like or how it moves. Do a couple of rounds of this activity and then have students sit down.

6. On chart paper, recreate Contributions Everywhere (RM 4.1). Review the Key Terms *contribution*. Ask students to help you identify the contributions of Indigenous peoples in the story (legends and constellations). Record these in the second column. Add other contributions like hockey, popcorn, and kayaks (can be found in Keoke and Porterfield's *Encyclopedia of American Indian Contributions to the World*).

7. In the first column, have students add contributions that they make at school and at home. You may have to prompt them with examples (e.g., being a good friend, taking care of a pet, sharing a snack, working hard in class, helping a classmate, putting up their sky picture).

8. Have a brief discussion as to why it is important to contribute. What does contributing feel like?

9. Give each student a copy of Contributions Everywhere (RM 4.1). Ask students to complete the columns by adding at least two new contributions in each column. Make sure there are resources available for them to search (e.g., variety of books, Internet).

Consolidation

- Once students have completed their organizer, bring their attention back to you by repeating the bodily-kinesthetic activity. This time, ask them to use their bodies to show the class one of their personal contributions from their list (e.g., "Show me what it looks like when you do the dishes"; "Show me what it looks like when you walk your dog"; "Show me what it looks like when you play hockey").

- Wrap up their learning by asking these questions:

  - What is your favourite part of the story in *Warren Whistles at the Sky*?

  - How do Warren and his Elders contribute to all of us?

  - Why is it important for us to make good contributions?

INTELLECTUAL

Assessment

For – Completion and descriptions of the sky pictures as prior knowledge.

As – Body movements mimicking the constellations and completion of Contributions Everywhere organizer.

Of – Responses to questions about the story and the concept of contributing.

EXTENSIONS

- Take your class to a planetarium or other venue that highlights constellations and sky phenomena.
- Do a virtual tour of a First Nation community, the businesses, and the variety of careers available.

CONTRIBUTIONS EVERYWHERE

Name: _____

Contributions that are personal to me (words or pictures below):	Contributions of Indigenous peoples (words or pictures below):

How do contributions make our lives better?

Grade Five Lesson Plan — Treaties

BACKGROUND INFORMATION FOR TEACHERS

Nearly the entire landmass of Canada is covered by treaties made between Indigenous peoples and the Crown (or representatives of the government of that time). Where you live or where your school is located is probably on treaty land. These treaties are recognized under the Constitution and reaffirm the existing and ongoing rights of the original peoples of Canada. Treaties are key to the relationship between Indigenous peoples and non-Indigenous peoples. An understanding and respect for the place and history of Indigenous peoples means understanding and respecting the treaties.

KEY TERMS

treaty: a formal agreement between parties; in Canada, treaties with Indigenous peoples were negotiated in nation-to-nation relationships.

wampum belt: symbol of an agreement between parties; shells sewn onto a belt represented various aspects of this agreement.

SPIRITUAL

Wampum belts are sacred and represent agreements made between peoples and nations. Wampum belts were kept by a skilled interpreter who was entrusted with the meaning of the belt. This drawing is based on a Mohawk belt called the "Women's Nomination Belt." It is a reminder that women are equals and have the right to help choose a chief in their clan.

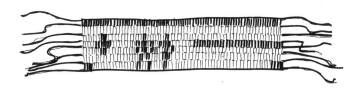

PHYSICAL

Time: 100 minutes

Materials/Resources

- map showing treaties of local area
- resources about and images of wampum belts (see pages 20 and 40)
- resources about treaties
- resources about Indigenous rites of passage
- projection device or smartboard
- *Treaty Tales: We Are All Treaty People* by Betty Lynxleg (2015)
- chart paper
- markers
- Treaties Venn Diagram (RM 5.1)

Considerations

- Find a map of the treaties made with Indigenous peoples in your area. Share with your students.
- Do not simplify the meaning of wampum belts. Use a reputable Indigenous source to provide the interpretation.

Suggested Adaptations by Subject

The Arts

Provide a variety of images of wampum belts to students. Have them identify the artistic techniques (line, space, colour, texture), feelings, and themes the wampum belts convey. Include the original meanings of each wampum belt for students to compare their predictions and reality.

Social Studies

Explore how earlier treaties have affected the lives of Indigenous peoples and non-Indigenous peoples today (e.g., land claims, rights/responsibilities, stewardship, resource protection). Focus on the treaty in your area.

Health and Physical Education

Include Indigenous rites of passage about becoming a responsible human being (e.g., teachings about menstruation, teachings about sexuality, teachings about fasting/vision quests). These values are inherent in treaties.

Science and Technology

Investigate the environmental effects of traditional Indigenous products compared to those of present-day technological society. For example:

CHILD'S DIAPER	
Indigenous	Traditionally, moss, which is disposable and recyclable, was used.
Today	Disposable diapers are made of plastic, wood fibres, polymers, and chemicals, and are not recyclable.

Mathematics

Find treaty areas and Indigenous sites of significance, using the cardinal directions (north, south, east, west). Incorporate common grid systems as part of this activity (e.g., treaty maps with coordinates indicated by letters, numbers, and/or directions).

EMOTIONAL

Learning Goal

To understand the role that we all have as treaty people living in Canada.

Step by Step

Minds-On

1. Project a copy of the Women's Nomination Belt from the Spiritual section onto a screen or your smartboard.
2. Review the Key Terms (*treaty* and *wampum belt*) with your students and place on your word wall. Let them know that the lesson today centres around treaties and wampum belts.
3. Ask students to examine the wampum belt and come up with predictions as to what they think the belt means.
4. Record their predictions on chart paper. Share with them the description of the belt from the Spiritual section. Discuss their predictions and the original Mohawk meaning.

During

1. Tell students they will be doing a bodily-kinesthetic activity about friendship and the terms of a friendship. Let them know you will be giving them a series of statements. They are to stand up if they agree with the statement and remain sitting if they disagree. Give students a variety of friendship scenarios, both good and bad (e.g., A friend is someone I can count on; A friend is someone who forces me to do things I don't want to do; A friend is someone who shares; A friend is someone who uses my things without permission).

2. Briefly discuss friendship with your students, using these questions:
    •   If you were to write up a contract on what a good friend is like, what would you put in that contract?
    •   What examples of good friendship would you include? What examples would be deal-breakers of that friendship (reasons you would stop being friends)?

3. After this discussion, show students the cover of the book *Treaty Tales: We Are All Treaty People*. Explain that treaties are contracts (agreements made between Indigenous peoples and the government as the representative of all citizens). For Indigenous peoples, the treaties set out what being a good citizen on their lands looked like, in a similar way to students' friendship contracts.

4. Read the book. Organize students into pairs or triads, and give each grouping a copy of the Treaties Venn Diagram (RM 5.1). Provide students with an example of a key learning about treaties from the book, and have them record this learning in the first circle of their Venn diagram. Prompt them for other key learnings, and have them record these on the diagram as well. Guide them in completing the first circle.

5. Direct students' attention to the second circle. Once again, give examples of what we can all do to honour the treaties (e.g., acknowledge the Indigenous land we live on, participate in National Treaty Week). Have students reflect on the book, as well as the friendship activity they did earlier. Ask them to complete this second part of the Venn diagram.

6. Do the bodily-kinesthetic activity again, but this time with a focus on the treaty relationship. Once again, let students know you will be providing a series of statements. They are to stand up if they agree with the statement and remain sitting if they disagree. Prompt students with statements from both the book and the classroom activities (e.g., a treaty is an agreement, a wampum belt is an agreement, we are all treaty people, we can break treaties if we want to, treaties have no meaning). Have them sit back down.

7. Ask students to analyze their Venn diagram and come up with one word or idea that is shared between both circles. Ask them to write this word or idea on their own diagram. Have one student from each group come forward and write this word or idea on your chart paper. Once all responses have been recorded, review these words or ideas and highlight the importance of their shared meanings (e.g., typical responses will be words like *respect, friendships, responsibility, future*).

Consolidation

•   Wrap up students' learning by asking these questions:
    •   What is your favourite part of the story in *Treaty Tales: We Are All Treaty People*?
    •   How do Neepin and her KooKoo teach us about treaties?
    •   Why is it important for us to do our part in honouring the treaties?

INTELLECTUAL

Assessment

For – Wampum belt predictions and meanings to establish prior knowledge and interest.

As – Class activity on terms of friendships and terms of treaties, as well as completion of Venn diagram on these concepts.

Of – Responses to questions regarding treaties and the importance of them to all of us.

EXTENSIONS

- Plan an event as part of National Treaty Week or attend an event (virtual or live).
- Invite a local Indigenous cultural resource person into your class to conduct a wampum belt workshop with students.

TREATIES VENN DIAGRAM

Name: _____

Identify one word or idea that both circles share: _____

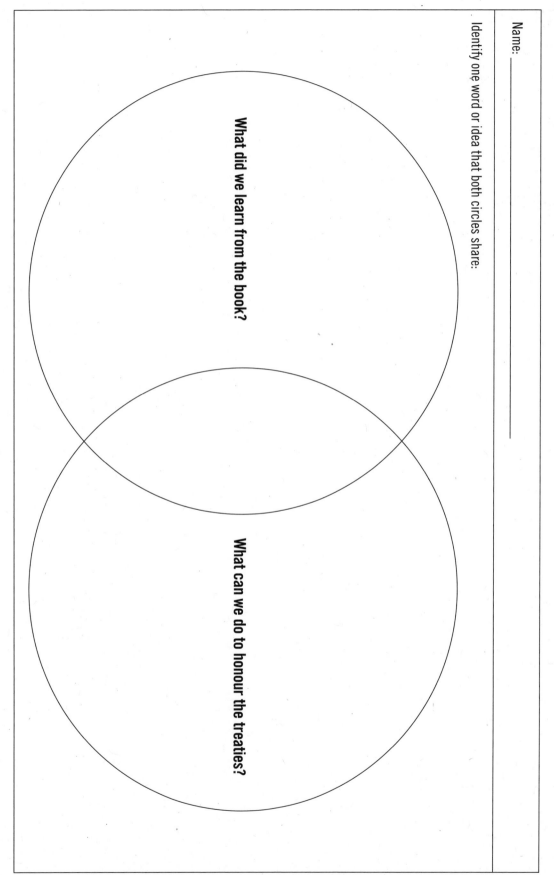

What did we learn from the book?

What can we do to honour the treaties?

Grade Six Lesson Plan — Residential Schools

BACKGROUND INFORMATION FOR TEACHERS

The last residential school closed in 1996. Approximately 150 000 First Nation, Métis, and Inuit children attended these schools. An estimated 1 in 25 of the children in these schools died. Traditional languages and customs were prohibited, hair was cut off or shaved, and children were required to wear uniforms of European design. The instruction of classes was in English, French, or Latin, and children who spoke in their own languages were often severely punished. Although some Indigenous people have reported that they had positive experiences, the majority did not. They frequently experienced physical abuse, sexual exploitation, and neglect.

KEY TERMS

residential schools: government-sponsored schools that were created to assimilate Indigenous children in Canada.

healing: the use of therapies or activities to help a person (or persons) become physically, emotionally, intellectually, and spiritually healthy.

SPIRITUAL

Indigenous students endured many forms of abuse. However, what has been called the "soul wound" continues to have the greatest impact today. The loss or hiding of original traditions, ceremonies, and languages created this wound. Indigenous children and the legacy of residential schools cannot be healed until this deep wound to the spirit is filled.

PHYSICAL

Time: 100 minutes

Materials/Resources

- resources about a local residential school, other residential schools, and reserves
- resources about events and developments that have affected Indigenous peoples, Indigenous models of self-concept, and statistics of Indigenous peoples (e.g., population, residential school survivors)
- *Shi-shi-etko* by Nicola I. Campbell (2005)
- chart paper
- markers
- sticky notes
- A Day of Memories (RM 6.1)
- pencil crayons

Considerations

Find a local resource on residential schools and healing-together strategies. Share with your students.

Do not use words like *inferior/superior* or *savage/civilized* unless you are sure your students have the maturity to process these concepts.

Suggested Adaptations by Subject

The Arts

Create musical compositions to accompany the stories you are reading about residential schools. Students should be able to connect the tone of the compositions and the creative choices to the mood of the scene or story.

Social Studies

Investigate other events and developments that have affected Indigenous peoples in Canada (e.g., the Indian Act; the reserve system; Indigenous protests, both current and historical; the national apology for residential schools).

Health and Physical Education

Explore Indigenous models of self-concept and the factors that affect the development of the whole person (physical, emotional, intellectual, spiritual). Have a guest speaker guide these discussions.

Science and Technology

Research the locations of residential schools and reserves and their conditions, including populations, health issues, housing, and land quality. Connect these conditions to the environmental issues that Indigenous peoples have been left with (e.g., tailings from mines, clear-cutting of forests, damming of lands). Explore solutions.

Mathematics

Develop an inquiry project related to statistics of Indigenous peoples (e.g., population, residential-school survivors, veterans, contributions). Make sure your students are able to read and write whole numbers. Arrange access to a variety of resources (e.g., Internet, books, news clips).

EMOTIONAL

Learning Goal

To appreciate the importance of memories and the impact of residential schools.

Step by Step

Minds-On

1. On chart paper, write the title "A Day to Remember." Let students know they are to think about a day or a celebration that was awesome. Provide them with a variety of prompts (e.g., birthday, holiday, trip with family, camping, track and field, school trip).

2. Give each student a sticky note. Have students record this day/celebration in word or picture form on the sticky note. Once they have completed this task, ask them to attach their sticky notes to your chart paper.

3. Review the days and celebrations that students have identified. Discuss what made these days/celebrations so special (e.g., fun, time spent with family/friends, good food).

4. Give each student another sticky note. Tell students you are going to be reading a story called *Shi-shi-etko*. Let them know that this story is directly related to the Key Terms (*residential schools* and *healing*). Review these terms with the class.

5. Set a reading goal with the students. Explain that they are going to record, using words or an image, a special moment that Shi-shi-etko describes in her last four days with her family.

During

1. Read the story. Pause at select sections where Shi-shi-etko describes her world (e.g., the wind, the mosquitoes, the bumblebees, her grandparents, the lake, her home). Remind students of their reading goal.

2. Once you finish reading, give students a chance to complete their sticky notes. On another piece of chart paper, write the title "Shi-shi-etko's Memories." Have students put their sticky notes on this chart paper. Review the memories of Shi-shi-etko that students have captured.

3. Discuss the similarities of memories between Shi-shi-etko and your students (e.g., typical answers will be family, friends, fun, food, home). Wrap up discussion by asking why Shi-shi-etko was so determined to keep these memories (e.g., leaving for residential school, where Indigenous children were not allowed to speak their own language and often did not see their families for years).

4. Give each student a copy of A Day of Memories (RM 6.1). Ask them to draw four events or activities that would make up a day for them to remember. How would the day begin and how would the day end?

Consolidation

- Once they have completed the activity, have students post their memory charts around the room. On a quick gallery walk, have them take a look at their peers' versions of a day to remember.

- Wrap up their learning by asking these questions:
  - What is your favourite part of the story in *Shi-shi-etko?*
  - How does Shi-shi-etko teach us to appreciate all things?
  - Why is it important for us to know about residential schools?

INTELLECTUAL

Assessment

For – Sticky notes with an example of a special memory or event as a base for students' prior knowledge.

As – Completion of a reading goal to capture a memory of the main character from the book, as well as drawing four scenes of their special day.

Of – Responses to questions about residential schools and what Shi-shi-etko teaches us.

EXTENSIONS

- Read other books about residential schools, and have students share their insights in a variety of formats (e.g., book reports, photo montages, dioramas, storyboards, poems).

- Invite a residential school survivor to the classroom to share age-appropriate aspects of their experiences.

A DAY OF MEMORIES

Name: _____

Caption:

Caption:

Caption:

Caption:

Grade Seven Lesson Plan — Blanket Exercise

BACKGROUND INFORMATION FOR TEACHERS

The KAIROS Blanket Exercise is an interactive and hands-on activity that teaches awareness and understanding of the history of Indigenous peoples in Canada. It is a highly effective tool that provides a space for you and your students to experience the losses and hopes of First Nation, Métis, and Inuit peoples. In order to guide this activity in an informed way, you must first complete a training exercise of eight short videos at: **https://www.kairosblanketexercise.org/resources/training-videos**. You will also have to request the scripts and the maps for this blanket exercise at: **https://www.kairosblanketexercise.org/resources/scripts** by completing a questionnaire.

Amazingly, the entire class has a role in this activity, and no one is left out. It creates a safe space for students to share their experiences and thoughts about Indigenous history. Although there is a level of preparation required for this exercise, it has so many benefits and is highly engaging.

KEY TERMS

truth: the real facts; to live in an authentic way that appreciates the journey and the destination.

reconciliation: to restore; the act of learning, relating, making amends, and moving forward.

SPIRITUAL

Truth and reconciliation is a journey of looking back, living in kindness today, and making changes for the future. It is about building relationships between citizens within a bond of healing and sacredness. This journey is action-oriented and moves beyond guilt; it focuses on honouring each other.

PHYSICAL

Time: 100 minutes

Materials/Resources

- local Elder or Métis Senator and a local Indigenous resource person
- Kairos Canada website: **https://www.kairoscanada.org/what-we-do/indigenous-rights/blanket-exercise**
- maps from Kairos Canada (Turtle Island, Treaties, and Aboriginal Lands Today)
- youth scripts from Kairos Canada
- blankets
- Blanket Exercise Reflections (RM 7.1)

Considerations

- Contact a local Elder or Métis Senator to be a key participant in this exercise.
- Do not avoid having difficult conversations about the history of Indigenous peoples. Do contact a local Indigenous resource person for assistance.

Suggested Adaptations by Subject

The Arts

Use dance and movement as a way to communicate the themes being learned in the blanket exercise (e.g., loss, hope, truth, reconciliation, residential schools, Indian Act, smallpox). Have students evaluate the strengths and challenges of their dance/movement.

History/Geography

Analyze the three maps that are part of this blanket exercise in more detail to examine shifts in power and changes in boundaries. Examine the issues (past and present) produced by these shifts and changes.

Health and Physical Education

Build upon interpersonal skills by examining bias toward Indigenous peoples and how students can respond to others who perpetuate these attitudes. Use the skills of empathy, setting boundaries, and education as tools for dealing with these types of situations.

Science and Technology

Using the map of Turtle Island, investigate the diversity of Indigenous perspectives on stewardship and sustainability. Show how these views can be used to take care of our Earth (animals and habitats).

Mathematics

Drawing on data from the scripts and maps in the blanket exercise, investigate these numbers and their relationships (e.g., fractions, decimals, percentages, ratios). This investigation will provide another lens for viewing the history of Indigenous peoples.

EMOTIONAL

Learning Goal

To be actively engaged in the history of Indigenous peoples in Canada.

Step by Step

Minds-On

1. Have all your students help you set up the blanket exercise (e.g., placing blankets on floor, putting scripts around and on the blankets).
2. Introduce the three maps. They show what North America looked like before European settlement (with 500 diverse nations), establish the breadth and number of treaties (covering nearly 100 percent of land in Canada), and depict the reality of Indigenous lands today (0.5 percent of their original territories).

During

1. Have students select a space to sit or stand, either on the blankets or at the edges. You can also prompt them to occupy certain areas. Give them some time to review the script they will read.
2. Begin this learning journey by following your script as the facilitator (or adapting the Kairos Canada script if you see the need – for time and/or student readiness reasons). Reminder: This journey involves you and your students together retelling the factual history of Indigenous peoples in Canada (and the United States).
3. Your script begins by asking students to sit on the blankets. This action represents the 500 nations before European settlement. A retelling of Indigenous history provides population facts and highlights the diversity of the 500 nations on Turtle Island.
4. Your script will then ask those students who have scripts to read their information, which is the story of settlement on Turtle Island by European settlers. Students will read various factual statements (e.g., the giving of smallpox-infested blankets to Indigenous peoples by the British as a way to eliminate them and secure lands).
5. Each time a fact is read, a blanket is folded up, and students are asked to leave that spot and find a place on the outside of the activity. Eventually nearly all the blankets will be folded up and a small number of students and blankets will remain. This small number of students that remain with the blankets represents the genocide of Indigenous peoples on Turtle Island.

Truth and Reconciliation in Canadian Schools

6. Your script concludes on a note of hope. The final scripts read by students highlight the strength of Indigenous peoples (e.g., Truth and Reconciliation Commission, IdleNoMore, revitalization of culture and language). As these scripts are read, some of the blankets are unfolded and students are asked to stand on them. The final picture shows that there is a movement for change happening on Turtle Island.

7. Once you complete this activity, have your students form a circle. Debrief them by allowing them to share (or not) what they have learned from the blanket exercise.

Consolidation

- Review the Key Terms (*truth* and *reconciliation*), and have each student complete Blanket Exercise Reflections (RM 7.1) as an exit form.
- Wrap up their learning by asking them to reflect on these questions:
  - What do our Key Terms tell us about the blanket exercise?
  - How does this blanket exercise deepen our knowledge of Indigenous history?
  - Why is it important for us to know these facts about our country?

INTELLECTUAL

Assessment

For – Review of the three maps as prior knowledge for the blanket exercise.

As – Engagement in the blanket exercise and sharing the impact of this activity.

Of – Completion of Blanket Exercise Reflections (RM 7.1) providing students' responses to questions about Indigenous history and the importance of learning it.

EXTENSIONS

- With your students, plan to carry out this blanket exercise with another class in your school, or with the school staff.
- Connect with another class that has participated in the blanket exercise (contacts are at the Kairos website) and engage in a social-action project.

BLANKET EXERCISE REFLECTIONS

Name: _____

Check the question you will respond to:

❑ What do our Key Terms tell us about the blanket exercise?

❑ How does this blanket exercise deepen our knowledge of Indigenous history?

❑ Why is it important for us to know these facts about our country?

Put your reflection here. Choose the form that suits your reflection — an image, paragraph, web, poem, key points, more questions, other.

Grade Eight Lesson Plan — National Celebrations

BACKGROUND INFORMATION FOR TEACHERS

In 1995, two events took place that led to the establishment of National Aboriginal Day in Canada. First, respected Elder Elijah Harper (who was chairing the Sacred Assembly, a national conference of Indigenous and non-Indigenous activists) called for a national day to celebrate Indigenous contributions. Second, the report released by the Royal Commission on Aboriginal Peoples also called for a designated national day for Indigenous recognition. The following year – 1996 – then-Governor General of Canada, Romeo LeBlanc, proclaimed June 21 as National Aboriginal Day each year (it was changed to National Indigenous Peoples Day, June 21, 2017). The date was chosen because it is usually the summer solstice, representing a sacred time and seasonal shift in the lives of First Nation, Métis, and Inuit peoples.

KEY TERMS

proclamation: an official and public announcement that addresses a vital matter of national importance.

solstice: a time of the year when the sun is at its lowest or its highest point at noon (also known as the shortest or longest day of the year). There are two solstices: winter, around December 22, and summer, around June 21.

SPIRITUAL

The solstice is regarded as sacred. Indigenous peoples' ancestral knowledge comes from the teachings of Mother Earth. The celebration at the right is a time to honour the changing of spring to summer. The regalia worn by these traditional dancers commemorates the land and her knowledge.

PHYSICAL

Time: *100 minutes (*for selection and initial planning phase only)

Materials/Resources

- National Indigenous Peoples Day website of Indigenous and Northern Affairs Canada, providing background, a list of events across the country, and learning resources: **https://www.aadnc-aandc.gc.ca/eng/1100100013248/1100100013249**
- crunchers from National Indigenous Day Learning Resources: **https://www.aadnc-aandc.gc.ca/eng/1302806502670/1302806682384**
- pencil crayons
- scissors
- computer lab (or class smartware for Macs, iPads, or other devices)
- access to the Internet
- National Indigenous Peoples Day Reflections (RM 8.1)

Considerations

- Connect with a local Indigenous organization that plans National Indigenous Peoples Day festivities. Share your intentions with them of planning an event with your students.
- Do not avoid conversations about the term *Aboriginal,* which was the used until 2017 to designate the day. Investigate this word and the self-identification names of local nations with your students.

Suggested Adaptations by Subject

The Arts

Identify the various types of music performed at National Indigenous Peoples Day events (e.g., big drum, hand drums, throat singing, fiddling, rapping). Compare and contrast these types with traditional and contemporary genres.

History/Geography

Plot on a map the National Indigenous Peoples Day events that are planned across the country. Describe the spatial patterns in those cities/communities (e.g., scattered, linear, clustered) and how the environments have been affected by these settlements (i.e., cities/communities).

Health and Physical Education

Investigate the movement skills and concepts (e.g., transfer of weight and rotations, static and dynamic balance, locomotor movements) of Indigenous dancers at National Indigenous Peoples Day celebrations.

Science and Technology

Identify the various systems required to plan and implement a National Indigenous Peoples Day celebration (e.g., body systems, mechanical systems, Indigenous leadership systems, mass transit systems).

Mathematics

Research the geometric properties of the designs on various dancers' regalia at National Indigenous Peoples Day celebrations (e.g., quadrilaterals, triangles, circles). Describe these designs using mathematical terminology (e.g., faces, vertices, edges, translations, reflections).

EMOTIONAL

Learning Goal

To research and plan an activity for National Indigenous Peoples Day.

Step by Step

Minds-On

1. Provide each student with a copy of the cruncher. Give them some time to colour their cruncher.
2. Have students cut and fold the crunchers, and let them play in pairs, triads, or quads. Each cruncher has interesting facts and information about Canada's Indigenous peoples.
3. Have each student share an interesting fact.

During

1. Take your class to the computer lab or provide each student with class smartware (e.g., Macs, iPads).
2. Ask students to go to the Plan for National Indigenous Peoples Day at: https://www.aadnc-aandc.gc.ca/eng/1100100013331/1100100013332. Ask them to review the suggested activities.
3. Have each student email you an activity from this page that they would like to see happen and would like to be involved in planning.
4. While you are tallying the suggested activities, send your students to the main National Aboriginal Day (NAD) page at:
   https://www.aadnc-aandc.gc.ca/eng/1100100013248/1100100013249. Ask them to investigate the links there (e.g., Indigenous and northern success stories, NAD on Flickr, #NADCanada on Twitter).
5. Share the top three results of your tally on National Indigenous Peoples Day activities that the class has selected. Discuss the strengths and challenges of each choice (e.g., impact, fun, time, cost). After this conversation, have students resubmit a choice from the list of the top three.

6. While you are doing the final tally, send students back to the main National Indigenous Peoples Day page to investigate the links.

7. Share the final choice of an activity that you and your class will plan for National Indigenous Peoples Day.

8. Start the planning process. This will vary depending on the activity selected by the class.

Consolidation

- Review the Key Terms (*proclamation* and *solstice*).

- Have each student complete National Indigenous Peoples Day Reflections (RM 8.1) as an exit form:

- Wrap up this section of their learning by reflecting on these questions:

  - What do the Key Terms tell us about National Indigenous Peoples Day?

  - How does this national day build relationships between people and communities?

  - Why is it important for us to plan an activity that honours Indigenous peoples?

INTELLECTUAL

Assessment

For – Cruncher activity with Indigenous facts to establish prior knowledge.

As – Research, evaluation, and voting on an activity for the entire class to plan for National Indigenous Peoples Day.

Of – Responses to selected questions about National Indigenous Peoples Day.

EXTENSIONS

- With your students, involve another class at your school and/or the parent school council to be a part of this celebration (e.g., taking on a role at the event – volunteering, setting up an information booth).

- Submit your class's performance or presentation as part of your contribution to another National Indigenous Peoples Day event.

NATIONAL INDIGENOUS PEOPLES DAY REFLECTIONS

Name: _____

Check the question you will respond to:

❏ What do the Key Terms tell us about National Indigenous Peoples Day?

❏ How does this national day build relationships between people and communities?

❏ Why is it important for us to plan an activity that honours Indigenous peoples?

Put your reflection here. Choose the form that suits your reflection – an image, paragraph, web, poem, key points, more questions, or other.

Grade Nine Lesson Plan — Making A Difference

BACKGROUND INFORMATION FOR TEACHERS

Indigenous peoples do not enjoy the same level of funding and services that their non-Indigenous counterparts receive. Indigenous children, youth, and families receive less funding in key areas like education, health, child welfare, and in their access to opportunities. This deficiency in funding and disregard for Indigenous peoples has resulted in higher rates of food insecurity, at-risk environments, and poor educational facilities. It is important that equity, respect, and the needs of Indigenous children are made a priority in Canada. Our children, youth, and families have the right to be able to pursue their dreams and live happily in their own lands.

KEY TERMS

racism: a belief that a particular race is superior to another; the act of discriminating against another race in multiple ways (e.g., language, social media, policies).

equity: fairness; having equal access to quality of life regardless of background; challenging and removing barriers.

SPIRITUAL

Every Indigenous nation has a word that describes a child. In Anishinaabe, the word is *Binoojiinhs,* but the meaning is much deeper and richer. *Binoojiinhs* means "raising little spirits," which elevates the view that we take of our children. It means that an entire community is responsible for this sacred being and his or her quality of life.

PHYSICAL

Time: 150 minutes (2 periods)

Materials/Resources

- Native Hip Hop website, a showcase for indigenous rap and hip-hop around the world: **http://www.nativehiphop.net/**
- First Nations Child & Family Caring Society of Canada website: **https://fncaringsociety.com/7-free-ways-make-difference**
- computer lab (or class smartware for Macs, iPads, or other devices)
- access to the Internet
- short dramatic works about Indigenous children, youth, and families (e.g., *Toronto at Dreamer's Rock* by Drew Hayden Taylor, *Where the Blood Mixes* by Kevin Loring)
- sticky notes
- markers
- Research Sheet (RM 9.1)

Considerations

- Know the backgrounds of your students, especially in this activity. You do not want Indigenous students to feel singled out.
- Do not avoid conversations about bias and stereotypes. Make sure to set the ground rules for respectful discussions.

Suggested Adaptations by Subject

English

Identify the messages portrayed or implied about Indigenous peoples, especially children and youth, in various media (e.g., social media, news, magazines, advertisements, products in stores). Examine the effects of these messages.

Canadian and World Studies

Select one or more development projects in or near Indigenous communities, and analyze their effects, both negative and positive, on the community (especially children and youth) and on traditional ways of life (e.g., mining exploration, pipeline projects, hydroelectric dams, residential housing developments, increased carbon emissions in the world and climate change).

Health and Physical Education

Investigate holistic models of health that use traditional Indigenous healing methods (e.g., invite a knowledgeable speaker such as an Elder, Métis Senator, or health professional; research a text or website). Analyze how these models reflect the health of Indigenous children and youth (and potentially themselves).

Guidance and Career Education

Research and identify community resources that are available to Indigenous children, youth, and families. Explain their purposes and how they can be accessed (e.g., friendship centres, Indigenous health access centres, Better Beginnings [in Ontario], healing lodges).

The Arts

Explore and interpret short dramatic works about Indigenous children, youth, and families, especially the issues they face (*Toronto at Dreamer's Rock* by Drew Hayden Taylor, *Where the Blood Mixes* by Kevin Loring). Develop personal responses to these works.

EMOTIONAL

Learning Goal

To investigate ways to make a difference in the lives of Indigenous children and youth.

Step by Step

Minds-On

1. Give each student a sticky note. Ask students to record (in words or images) something they cannot live without. Once they have done so, have them place this sticky note somewhere in the classroom. Ask them to stand in front of their sticky note. Explain they will be doing a gallery walk of the things they cannot live without. The entire class will move in the same direction and see what their peers had to say.

2. Once students have had a chance to see one another's comments, ask them to return to their seats. Review the key things they cannot live without.

3. Hold a discussion about the question "Are there people here in Canada who do go without?" Typically, students will allude to particular neighbourhoods and groups. Be prepared to assist them in using more respectful terms as part of this discussion.

DURING

1. Let students know they are going to view a music video from Indigenous youth. Their task is to think about the messages and images being presented in the video and lyrics. Play one of the videos from the hip-hop link in the Materials/Resources section.

2. Ask students to take another sticky note and record the key message or image they received from the video and/or song. Repeat the same gallery walk activity as in Minds-On.

3. Provide a mini-lesson (five minutes) about the challenges that Indigenous children and youth face (e.g., treaties not being honoured, systemic racism).

4. Hand out copies of Research Sheet (RM 9.1). Let students know they have the choice of working individually or as pairs in this task. Review the topic options they will be researching. Explain that each of these topics is an initiative aimed at supporting

Indigenous children, youth, and families (e.g., Many Hands, One Dream is a collaborative initiative aimed at building a new vision of health that has children, youth, and families at its core). Assign the six topics in equal numbers to the class.

5. Take your students to the computer lab or give out the smartware. Give them the link (**https://fncaringsociety.com/7-free-ways-make-difference**) from the Materials/Resources section. Prompt students to focus on researching their particular topic at this site. This activity will take them into the next class (or period) that you have with them.

6. Once your students have done their research, ask them to summarize their findings in one paragraph or in four clear points. Post these summaries by topic around the classroom. Review the six topics as researched by the class.

Consolidation

- Review the Key Terms (*racism* and *equity*).
- Wrap up this section of student learning by reflecting on these questions:
    - What did we learn about Indigenous children and youth through this activity?
    - How do the Key Terms relate to the six topics that you researched?
    - Why is it important for us to reflect on what we need and what others need?

INTELLECTUAL

Assessment

For – Sticky notes that describe what students need and a discussion about those people who go without.

As – Discussion of the images and messages from Indigenous youth. Completion of research activity on ways to make change.

Of – Responses to questions that reflect equity, change, and social action.

EXTENSIONS

- Select one of these initiatives and carry it out with your class or school.
- Work with a local Indigenous organization to be part of one of these events.

RESEARCH SHEET

Name: _____

Circle the topic (initiative) you have been assigned from "Free Ways to Make a Difference":

❏ *I Am a Witness*

❏ *Jordan's Principle*

❏ *Shannen's Dream for Safe and Comfy Schools*

❏ *Touchstones of Hope*

❏ *Child and Youth Engagement*

❏ *Many Hands, One Dream*

Go to the link provided by your teacher. Describe the initiative and how you can make a difference.

Grade Ten Lesson Plan — Project of Heart

BACKGROUND INFORMATION FOR TEACHERS

There are many ways to engage in truth and reconciliation activities and movements across Canada. Project of Heart (**http://projectofheart.ca/**) is one such activity. Its purpose is reconciliation and learning about the effects and legacy of residential schools, but the responsibility to change together is the spirit that drives it. It provides amazing examples of the power, strength, and impact that our youth have as they plan and implement social-action events for both Indigenous and non-Indigenous healing.

As your students work through these activities, the voices of residential-school survivors and youth across this vast land will be a lasting memory for them. It will also inspire them to take action in some form.

KEY TERMS

genocide: the deliberate destruction (in whole or in part) of a people (usually defined as an ethnic, national, racial, or religious group); a coordinated plan to destroy a nation or people.

responsibility: being accountable for one's actions; carrying out an act that is morally responsible and just; making change in areas of equity and inclusion.

SPIRITUAL

Every Indigenous nation has teachings that describe the life stage or rites of passage of an adolescent. In traditional Anishinaabe societies, the life stage of an adolescent is called "the wandering life." It is a time when our young people (aged 14 to 21) challenge, question, and seek new experiences. It is a time of testing and discovery. All of these explorations shape the person spiritually, physically, emotionally, and intellectually. Teachings through peers, the media, and other influences contribute in positive and negative ways to who adolescents are becoming.

PHYSICAL

Time: 150 minutes (2 periods)

Materials/Resources

- media text for Project of Heart activity
- Elder or Métis Senator
- resources about healing and wellness careers in Indigenous communities
- fundraising website GoFundMe: **https://ca.gofundme.com/**
- Project of Heart website: **http://projectofheart.ca/**
- computer lab (or class smartware for Macs, iPads, or other devices)
- access to the Internet
- various art supplies for mixed-media, printmaking, painting, sculpture, drawing activities
- sticky notes
- markers
- Project of Heart (RM 10.1)

Considerations

- Do acknowledge the strengths of Indigenous peoples, despite the many challenges that will be discussed.
- Do not assume that all websites about Indigenous people have accurate information. Review the website and its editorial processes.

Suggested Adaptations by Subject

English

Examine why different media texts about residential schools – apologies, speeches, songs, social media, news, magazines – have received different responses from different groups (e.g., the National Apology and its effects on survivors, social media and youth). Select one of these media texts for a Project of Heart activity.

Canadian and World Studies

Identify primary sources (e.g., photographs, statistics, diaries, letters, maps, treaties) and secondary sources (newspapers, films, books, articles) on residential school history since 1914. Create a textual piece for a Project of Heart activity.

Health and Physical Education

Build interpersonal skills in the areas of respect and relationships by listening to the teachings of an Elder or Métis Senator. Apply these skills and teachings in a social-action campaign or Project of Heart activity.

Guidance and Career Education

Find information on healing and wellness careers in Indigenous communities and with Indigenous peoples. Connect these careers to the reconciliation process through building relationships.

The Arts

Create art works that communicate feelings and emotions around residential-school effects, histories, and Indigenous resilience. Use various techniques (e.g., mixed-media, printmaking, painting, sculpture, drawing) and the work of Indigenous artists as inspiration. (See **http://ccca. concordia.ca/artists/index.html?languagePref=en&** for an extensive list in alphabetical order.)

EMOTIONAL

Learning Goal

To explore Project of Heart activities and connect with another secondary school involved in Project of Heart.

Step by Step

Minds-On

1. As your students come into class, put up the website GoFundMe (**https://ca.gofundme. com/**) on your screen or smartboard. Introduce your students to this site by reviewing its purpose and the many projects that are seeking funding.

2. Give each student a sticky note and markers. On your smartboard (or screen) go through some of the projects at GoFundMe (images and icons on the home page reflect particular types of projects such as animal centres, medical needs, other). Have each student write down a cause, item, or topic that he/she would support.

3. Once students have recorded their choice on the sticky notes, have them place the notes on the walls in the classroom. Ask students to safely walk around the room and check out what their peers have listed. Once they have viewed one another's sticky notes, have them return to their seats.

4. On the GoFundMe site, put in the name of your community or nearby city, and search for the most recent campaigns in your area. Take about five minutes to check out the causes (some will be quite serious; others will be questionable).

5. Discuss the importance of fundraising, volunteerism, and social action.

During

1. Let students know they will be researching a social action website called Project of Heart, dedicated to relationship-building between Indigenous and non-Indigenous peoples. Tell them this process will be one of discovery that will lead to developing a relationship with another high school.

2. Provide your students with copies of Project of Heart (RM 10.1). Have them work individually or in pairs on this task. Review the sections from the Project of Heart website that they will be researching. Assign the eight topics in equal numbers to the class.

3. Take your students to the computer lab or give out the smartware. Give students the link (**http://projectofheart.ca/**) from the Materials/Resources section. Prompt them to research their topic at this site. This activity will take them into the next class (or period) that you have with them.

4. Once your students have done their research, ask them to summarize their findings in two paragraphs or in eight clear points. Post these summaries by topic around the classroom. Review the eight topics as researched by the class.

5. Revisit the eight topics, and highlight those that involve projects and activities led by secondary students. Take a poll (top three) of these groups or projects that interest them the most.

6. Discuss the strengths and challenges of each of these three projects. Take another poll and identify the top group or project out of the three.

7. As a class, develop a one-page letter or email to the other secondary-school class (represents the top project selected from Project of Heart) that:
   - introduces your class
   - describes what students admire about the Project of Heart activity done by the other students
   - expresses your class's wish to connect with a secondary class from their school (either to establish a cordial connection and discuss social action, or to engage in a collaborative social-action project that is consistent with the Project of Heart mandate)
   - includes a photo of your whole class (if you have permission to do so)

8. Send this letter and photo to the secondary school administrator (name and school is listed and easily accessible via Google search). This is your first contact for school board protocol reasons. The administrator (principal or vice-principal) can forward this request to the appropriate teacher at recipient's school.

9. Share the response once you have received one, and develop a plan to either set up a discussion group or proceed to plan a project.

Consolidation

- Review the Key Terms (*genocide* and *responsibility*).
- Wrap up this section of student learning by reflecting on these questions:
  - What did we learn about Project of Heart through this activity?
  - How do the Key Terms connect to the many social-action projects at this site?
  - Why is it important (or not) for us to educate ourselves and engage in social action?

INTELLECTUAL

Assessment

For – Exploring and discussing the many causes that are personal and on social media.

As – Completing the research activity on Project of Heart and conducting correspondence with a secondary school involved in Project of Heart.

Of – Responding to questions that reflect concepts of genocide and responsibility.

EXTENSIONS

- Investigate the upcoming events at Project of Heart and participate in one.
- Work with a local Indigenous community to learn about its traditions and lived realities.

Name: _____

Check the section you have been assigned at the Project of Heart website:

❑ Home

❑ What Is Project of Heart?

❑ Our History

❑ Project of Heart in the News

❑ British Columbia

❑ Ontario

❑ Saskatchewan

❑ Quebec

Grade Eleven Lesson Plan — No More Stolen Sisters

BACKGROUND INFORMATION FOR TEACHERS

Indigenous women face more violence more often than their non-Indigenous counterparts. They are three times more likely to experience violence and six times more likely to be murdered. The stereotypes of Indigenous women as objects, "easy" or sexually available, and less than human have contributed to these alarming numbers. The crucial issue of missing and murdered Indigenous women did not appear on the national radar until about 2007, although it had always been on the minds and in the lives of the families who lost their daughters, nieces, mothers, and sisters.

The fundamental questions for our society should be: How is it that more than 1200 Indigenous women have gone missing and we have only recently learned about it? What led to this situation being overlooked for many decades? And why do we need to listen and change together?

KEY TERMS

sexism: beliefs, attitudes, and practices that indicate one gender (usually male) is dominant or superior; being denied quality of life and access to opportunities because of one's gender (usually female).

courage: the ability to do or face something that you know is difficult or dangerous, including ideas and practices that are inhumane, and institutions and societal forces that contribute to these ideas and practices.

SPIRITUAL

ELDER JOSEPHINE MANDAMIN

Elder Josephine Mandamin of Wikwemikong First Nation, Ontario, is known as the "Water Walker." Since 2003 she has conducted 13 Water Walks around the perimeters of all five Great Lakes, as well as along other lakes and rivers in Canada and the United States. She has inspired a generation of women to care for the water.

Every Indigenous nation has teachings about the sacredness and role of women. The Elders share teachings about our grandmother, the Moon, and how she affects the tides and the cycles of women. Women are to be honoured every day as the givers of life.

In Anishinaabe societies, women are the keepers of the water, since without it we cannot survive. They are responsible for the lifeblood of Mother Earth.

PHYSICAL

Time: 150 minutes (2 periods)

Materials/Resources

- access to Elder or Métis Senator
- access to counsellors and support persons
- media texts and advertisements that focus on Indigenous peoples
- resources about the social determinants of health for Indigenous peoples
- resources about social institutions for Indigenous peoples
- copies of artwork that are models of Indigenous activism supporting missing and murdered women (e.g., *Walking With Our Sisters*)
- Amnesty International Canada website: **https://www.amnesty.ca/our-work/campaigns/no-more-stolen-sisters**
- computer lab (or class smartware for Macs, iPads, or other devices)
- access to the Internet
- No More Stolen Sisters (RM 11.1)

- various images of women (find and include a diverse range)
- sticky notes
- markers

Considerations

- Contact a local Indigenous Elder or Métis Senator and find out what his/her teachings are about women. Share with students.
- Provide your students with access to and contact information for counsellors and support persons. This lesson is about violence against women and may be a trigger for some.

Suggested Adaptations by Subject

English

Collect a variety of media texts and advertisements about Indigenous peoples. Analyze the perspectives and biases they demonstrate. Comment on the beliefs, values, and possible stereotypes that are being promoted.

Canadian and World Studies

On issues related to Indigenous peoples, investigate the perspectives of bystanders and upstanders (e.g., what reasons or motivations do people give for choosing to get involved – or not – in political and social action with and for Indigenous peoples?).

Health and Physical Education

The social determinants of health – the conditions in the places where people live, learn, work, and play – affect a wide range **of health** risks and outcomes. Research the social determinants of health for Indigenous peoples. List culturally appropriate programs and strategies in your area that can help address the wellness of Indigenous peoples (e.g., healing lodges, restorative justice programs, friendship centres). Select and research one of these programs and/or strategies.

Social Sciences and Humanities

Describe the social institutions (e.g., clans, dodems, roles) of one local First Nation, one Inuit community or group, and one provincial Métis Nation or community. Analyze the importance of their social institutions to the process of reconciliation.

The Arts

Explore various artworks that are models of activism for and with Indigenous peoples and their rights (e.g., *Walking With Our Sisters*, a commemorative art installation for missing and murdered Indigenous women of Canada and the United States, by Christi Belcourt, **http://walkingwithoursisters.ca/**; the Reconciliation Pole carved by Haida Nation hereditary chief James Hart). Using these artworks as inspiration, have students modify elements and create an artwork dedicated to a cause.

EMOTIONAL

Learning Goal

To investigate the issue of missing and murdered Indigenous women and engage in a class social-action activity.

Step by Step

Minds-On

1. Post images of women (make sure there is a diverse range) around the classroom. As students come into class, have them examine the images you have provided. Ask them to think about the potential messages that the images are transmitting.

2. Hold a brief discussion about these images and what their meaning might be for different people (possible or expected effects, potential behaviour toward).

3. Let students know they will be watching a four-minute video, "Highway of Tears," about missing and murdered Indigenous women at: **http://www.cbc.ca/radio/thecurrent/ features/missingandmurdered/vr** (the link provides several ways to view it).

4. Show this short documentary on your screen or smartboard.

5. Give each student a sticky note and markers. Have them record a thought or image about the video they have just viewed. Ask them to post these around the room. Take a couple of minutes to have your students walk around the room and review what their peers have written or drawn.

6. Hold a brief discussion about students' words and images.

During

1. Let students know they will be researching a website, Amnesty International Canada, that is dedicated to human rights and social justice.

2. Provide your students with copies of No More Stolen Sisters (RM 11.1). Have them work individually or in pairs on this task. Review the sections from the Amnesty International Canada website they will be researching. Assign the six topics in equal numbers to the class.

3. Take your students to the computer lab or give out the smartware. Give students the link to Amnesty International Canada from the Materials/Resources section. Have them research their topic at this site. This activity will take them into the next class (or period) you have with them.

4. Once students have done their research, ask them to summarize their findings in three paragraphs or in 12 clear points. Post these summaries by topic around the classroom. Review the six topics as researched by the class.

5. Hold a discussion on social-action activities students can do today (or in this semester) as suggested on the Amnesty International Canada website. From the discussion, develop a plan (or a student working committee) to carry out the social-action activity.

Consolidation

- Review the Key Terms (*sexism* and *courage*).
- Wrap up this section of their learning by reflecting on these questions:
  - What did we learn about Indigenous women through these activities?
  - How do the Key Terms relate to the six topics that you researched?
  - Why is it important for us to explore this issue and do something about it?

INTELLECTUAL

Assessment

For – Discussion about the images of women. Sticky note activity of the key messages from the video "Highway of Tears."

As – Completion of research on No More Stolen Sisters and selection of social action activity.

Of – Responses to questions about Indigenous women, sexism, and the courage to change.

EXTENSIONS

- Host a screening of the feature-length film *Highway of Tears* (2015) available through Amnesty International.
- Connect with a local Indigenous organization and participate in a water walk with your class.

NO MORE STOLEN SISTERS

Name: _____

Check the section you have been assigned at the Amnesty International Canada website:

❑ What Can I Do?

❑ Resources

❑ Human Rights Crisis

❑ Solutions

❑ Indigenous Women and Resource Development

❑ Latest Developments

Go to the link provided by your teacher. Review your section (including information, action items, photos, news) and describe below.

Grade Twelve Lesson Plan — Moving Beyond Acknowledgments and Apologies

BACKGROUND INFORMATION FOR TEACHERS

Many acknowledgments and apologies have recently dominated the conversations between and about Indigenous and non-Indigenous peoples. It is time to move beyond this behaviour and into taking action as human beings committed to a greater good – that of a more just society (including the protection of other-than-human-beings). Social action for justice comes from a place where we *feel* (we are bonded by emotions and spirit) and thus deeply relate to each other's loss, grief, hope, and happiness.

This last lesson plan is based upon the formation of an authentic relationship (preferably long-term) between your class and an Indigenous community, group, organization, cause, family, or person. This activity requires the most work and the most time. It will go beyond the school term for some (and hopefully most) of your students.

KEY TERMS

authentic: not false; genuine, true, and purposeful.

action: an act or deed; the process of doing something (ideally for the greater good).

SPIRITUAL

Every Indigenous nation has teachings and stories about humour. Each nation has characters in the legends that embody this important value. Humour and the gift of laughter is not only a social norm among Indigenous peoples; it is a sign of trust. Teasing (in a respectful manner) is a signal that friendship is on its way. Steps toward mutual acceptance require time and work. Laughter is a healing medicine that is shared.

Waynaboozhoo

PHYSICAL

Time: 150 minutes (2 periods)

Materials/Resources

- *Red Rising Magazine*: **http://redrisingmagazine.ca/** (an open forum for Indigenous news, artwork, poetry, and essays, produced quarterly by an Indigenous youth collective based in Winnipeg)
- interviews of and by Indigenous writers
- resources about human rights laws of Canada
- resources about the role of sport in Indigenous society (**http://www.lnhl.ca/; http://www.naigcouncil.com/**)
- resources about Indigenous fashion by Indigenous designers (e.g., Dorothy Grant, Tishynah Buffalo, Curtis Oland)
- access to Indigenous drama productions, live or virtual (e.g., Native Earth Performing Arts in Toronto; Talking Stick Festival in Vancouver, British Columbia)
- access to the Internet
- computer lab (or class smartware for Macs, iPads, or other devices)
- A Letter to the Next Class (RM 12.1)

Considerations

- If you have an Indigenous student council (or rep), ask them to provide advice. For example, ask if they can come and speak, if the class can come to them, or if they can recommend a person to come and speak about local Indigenous nations.
- Do not undervalue the importance of gifting as part of establishing a formal relationship with Indigenous peoples (e.g., tobacco ties, food, honoraria).

Suggested Adaptations by Subject

English

Find interviews with Indigenous writers (e.g., playwrights, poets, news articles, bloggers), and examine the art and craft of their practices, processes, and beliefs (e.g., Janet Rogers – Mohawk/Tuscarora from Six Nations, Ontario; Joanne Arnott – Métis from Portage la Prairie, Manitoba).

Canadian and World Studies

Research the importance of human rights laws in Canada (and also the contradictions in real life) as they apply to Indigenous peoples. Compare and contrast these laws, including the Charter of Rights, and evaluate their effectiveness.

Health and Physical Education

Investigate the role of sport in Indigenous society and how it has evolved. Examine the issues, trends, impact, and role of sport (e.g., the Little NHL – Native Hockey League – at: **http://www.lnhl.ca/**; the North American Indigenous Games at: **http://www.naigcouncil.com/**).

Social Sciences and Humanities

Find resources about Indigenous fashion by Indigenous designers (e.g., Dorothy Grant, Tishynah Buffalo, Curtis Oland). Use both primary resources, such as samples of designs, and secondary resources, including news articles and TV programs. Explore the designers' works, the textiles, and the impact of their designs. Compare these to the works of selected non-Indigenous designers who have used Indigenous designs and influences.

The Arts

Attend Indigenous drama productions – live or virtual – and analyze how the technology helps or hinders the creation of mood, tension, and connection to personal experiences (e.g., Native Earth Performing Arts in Toronto; Talking Stick Festival in Vancouver, British Columbia).

EMOTIONAL

Learning Goal

To connect with Indigenous peoples and form a relationship committed to reconciliation.

Step by Step

Minds-On

1. Take your students to the computer lab, or give each student class smartware (Macs, iPads, or other devices). Direct your students to the *Red Rising Magazine* website (**http://redrisingmagazine.ca/**). Provide them with an opportunity to explore the news, articles, poetry, videos, music, art, events, and live icons on their own without your direction.

2. Have students share, via large screen, what they found interesting about the magazine (e.g., voices of youth their age, perspectives on identity and sexuality, upcoming events in their area, music that needs to be heard).

3. Briefly discuss the commonalities and differences in experiences and worldview between themselves and the contributors. Ask: What can we learn from each other? Why is this learning important?

During

1. Team your students in pairs or triads (or they can work alone if they prefer). Guide them in researching local First Nation, Métis, and Inuit organizations, communities, or groups (e.g., who they are, where they are located, what they do). Have them submit their findings to you at the end of this class period.

2. Collate this information in one package for students. Give out the package to all students at the beginning of the next period.

3. Let your students know that this package contains information to help them connect to Indigenous peoples. It has the necessary contact and event information for you and your students to consider. Remind them that authentic relationships are part of reconciliation and that action is fundamental.

4. Set plans, either as individual or as a class, to pursue a connection, friendship, or relationship, or attend an event, with and for Indigenous peoples. The times and outcomes of this activity will vary.

Consolidation

- Review the Key Terms (*authentic* and *action*).
- Complete A Letter to the Next Class (RM 12.1) as part of an exit requirement for your course. Ask your students to include the advice, challenges, insights, and other information they would like to pass on to other students as part of pursuing relationships with Indigenous peoples.
- Wrap up this section of their learning by reflecting on these questions:
  - What have we learned through these activities in these last two periods?
  - How do the Key Terms relate to connecting with Indigenous peoples?
  - Why is it important for us to act (or not act)?

INTELLECTUAL

Assessment

For – Exploration and discussion of *Red Rising Magazine* content and contributors.

As – Research and establishment of connection with Indigenous peoples.

Of – Completion and submission of letter to other students.

EXTENSIONS

- Help out at an Indigenous feast with your Indigenous connection as part of a local event.
- Suggest to students that they offer to speak to other young adults about what they are learning.

A LETTER TO THE NEXT CLASS

Name: _____

My letter is written below on the birchbark scroll in a format of my choice (words, poetry, images, lyrics, point form, web, more questions to think about, other).

References

Alberta Aboriginal Services Branch & Learning and Teaching Resources Branch. *Our Words, Our Ways: Teaching First Nations, Métis and Inuit Learners*. Edmonton, AB: Alberta Education, 2005.

Barkwell, L. *Contributions Made by Métis People*. Winnipeg, MB: Louis Riel Institute, 2017.

Benton-Banai, E. *Anishinaabe Almanac: Living Through the Seasons*. M'Chigeeng, ON: Kenjgewin Teg Educational Institute, 2008.

Benton-Banai, E. *The Mishomis Book: The Voice of the Ojibway*. 2nd ed. Minneapolis: University of Minnesota Press, 2010.

Bradshaw Foundation. Petroglyphs and Pictographs from Canada. Retrieved from <**http://www.bradshawfoundation.com/canada/western_canada/index.php**>.

Canadian Encyclopedia. Totem Pole. Retrieved from http://www.thecanadianencyclopedia.ca/en/article/totem-pole/.

Canada's Historic Places. (2017). Majorville Cairn and Medicine Wheel. Retrieved from <**http://www.historicplaces.ca/en/rep-reg/place-lieu.aspx?id=15835**>.

Canadian Museum of History. (2017). Gateway to Aboriginal Heritage. Retrieved from <**http://www.historymuseum.ca/cmc/exhibitions/tresors/ethno/etb0170e.shtml**>.

DeLoatch, P. (2015). The Four Negative Sides of Technology. Retrieved from <**http://www.edudemic.com/the-4-negative-side-effects-of-technology/**>.

Deloria, V. *God Is Red: A Native View of Religion, 30th Anniversary Edition*. Golden, CO: Fulcrum Publishing, 2003.

Dion, S. *The Listening Stone, Learning From the Ontario Ministry of Education's First Nations, Métis and Inuit-Focused Collaborative Inquiry 2013–2014*. Oakville, ON: Council of Ontario Directors of Education (CODE), 2014.

Early Canadiana Online. (2017). Aboriginals: Treaties and Relations. Retrieved from <**https://web.archive.org/web/20150219015549/http://www.canadiana.ca/citm/themes/aboriginals_e.html**>.

First Nations Child & Family Caring Society of Canada. (2016). *Indigenous Contributions to North America and the World*. Ottawa.

First Nations & Indigenous Studies, University of British Columbia. (2017). Indigenous Foundations – The Indian Act. Retrieved from **http://indigenousfoundations.arts.ubc.ca/the_indian_act/**.

First Nations Education Steering Committee & First Nations Schools Association. (2015). *Indian Residential Schools & Reconciliation – Teacher Resource Guide*. Vancouver, BC.

Goldi Productions Ltd. (2017). Treaties & Cultural Change. Retrieved from <**http://firstpeoplesofcanada.com/fp_treaties/fp_treaties_two_views.html**>.

Goulais, B. (2006, December 13). Anishinaabe scrolls come full circle (Blog post). <**http://www.anishinaabe.ca/index.php/2006/12/13/Anishinaabe-scrolls-come-full-circle/**>.

Government of Northwest Territories, Government of Nunavut & Legacy of Hope Foundation. (2013). *The Residential School System in Canada: Understanding the Past – Seeking Reconciliation – Building Hope for Tomorrow (2nd Edition)*. Yellowknife, NT.

Government of Ontario. (2017). Ontario Proclaims First Week of November Treaties Recognition Week. Retrieved from <**https://news.ontario.ca/mirr/en/2016/05/ontario-proclaims-first-week-of-november-treaties-recognition-week.html**>.

Haudenosaunee Confederacy. (2017). Wampum. Retrieved from <http://haudenosauneeconfederacy.com/NewSite/Confederacy/wampum.html>.

Historica Canada. (n.d.). *Residential Schools in Canada – Education Guide.* Toronto.

Historica Canada. (2017). Indigenous Peoples: Treaties. Retrieved from <http://www.thecanadianencyclopedia.ca/en/article/aboriginal-treaties/>.

Indian and Northern Affairs Canada. (2010). *A History of Treaty-Making in Canada.* Gatineau, QC.

Indigenous and Northern Affairs Canada. (2017). Did you know? Retrieved from <http://www.aadnc-aandc.gc.ca/eng/1302807151028/1302807416851>.

_____. Part 2 – History of First Nations – Newcomer Relations. *First Nations in Canada.* Retrieved October 16, 2017 from: https://www.aadnc-aandc.gc.ca/eng/1307460755710/1307460872523#chp2.

_____. Fact Sheet: Aboriginal Self Government. Retrieved from http://www.aadnc-aandc.gc.ca/eng/1100100016293/1100100016294

Indigenous Corporate Training Inc. (2017). Working Effectively With Indigenous Peoples. Retrieved from <http://www.ictinc.ca/blog/indigenous-peoples-worldviews-vs-western-worldviews>.

Indigenous Works. (2017). Differences between traditional Indigenous cultures and mainstream Western cultures. Retrieved from <https://indigenousworks.ca/en/resources/getting-started/cultures>.

Inuit Tapiriit Kanatami. (2016). *National Inuit Suicide Prevention Strategy.* Ottawa.

Johnston, B. *Indian School Days.* Norman, OK: University of Oklahoma Press, 1988.

Joseph, B. (2017). 21 things you may not know about the Indian Act. Retrieved from <http://www.cbc.ca/news/indigenous/21-things-you-may-not-know-about-the-indian-act-1.3533613>.

Keoke, E.D., and K.M. Porterfield. American Indian Contributions to the World. New York: Checkmark Books, 2003.

Lackenbauer, P.W., J. Moses, R. S. Sheffield, & M. Gohier. *A Commemorative History of Aboriginal Peoples in the Canadian Military.* Ottawa: National Defence, n.d.

Land Claims Agreements Coalition. (2017). Modern Treaties. Retrieved from <http://www.landclaimscoalition.ca/modern-treaties/>.

Legacy of Hope Foundation. Where Are the Children? Website. Timeline – A History of the Residential School System in Canada. (2017, February 21). Retrieved from <http://wherearethechildren.ca/en>.

Métis Culture/Our Legacy. (2017). Métis Culture. Retrieved from <http://digital.scaa.sk.ca/ourlegacy/exhibit_metisculture>.

Natural Resources Canada. (2017). Indigenous Place Names. Retrieved from <http://www.nrcan.gc.ca/earth-sciences/geography/place-names/indigenous/19739>

Office of the Treaty Commissioner. (2017). Teaching Treaties in the Classroom. Retrieved from <http://www.otc.ca/resource/purchase/teaching_treaties_in_the_classroom.html?page=3>.

Richmond, C.A.M. & N. A. Ross. (2009). The determinants of First Nation and Inuit health: A critical population approach. *Health & Place, 15(2),* 403–411.

Robinson-Huron Treaty, 1850, Between Her Majesty the Queen and the Ojibwa Indians of Lake Huron. Retrieved from https://www.aadnc-aandc.gc.ca/eng/1100100028984/1100100028994.

Royal Alberta Museum. (2017). What Is a Medicine Wheel? Retrieved from <http://www.royalalbertamuseum.ca/research/culturalStudies/archaeology/faq.cfm>.

Smith-Gilman. S. (2015). Culture Matters: The Arts, The Classroom Environment and a Pedagogy of Entewate'Nikonri:sake : A Study in a First Nations Pre-School. *Canadian Review of Art Education: Research and Issues, 42*(2), 53–68.

Snively, G. & L. W. Williams. *Knowing Home: Braiding Indigenous Science with Western Science.* Victoria, BC: University of Victoria, 2016.

Stanford History Education Group. (2017). What Is an "Inquiry Lesson"? Retrieved from
<http://teachinghistory.org/teaching-materials/teaching-guides/24123>.

Statistics Canada. (2017a). Aboriginal languages in Canada – Census Program – Statistics Canada. Retrieved
from <http://www12.statcan.gc.ca/nhs-enm/2011/as-sa/99-011-x/99-011-x2011003_1-eng.cfm>.

Statistics Canada. (2017b). Statistics by Subject: Aboriginal peoples – Statistics Canada. Retrieved from
<http://www.statcan.gc.ca/eng/subjects/aboriginal_peoples>.

Statistics Canada. (2017c). Aboriginal Peoples in Canada: First Nations People, Métis and Inuit. Retrieved
from <http://www12.statcan.gc.ca/nhs-enm/2011/as-sa/99-011-x/99-011-x2011001-eng.cfm>.

St. Denis, V. *A Study of Aboriginal Teachers' Professional Knowledge and Experience in Canadian Schools*.
Ottawa: Canadian Teachers' Federation, 2010.

The Inuit Impact/Inuit Cultural Online Resource (2017). The Inuit Impact. Retrieved from
<http://icor.ottawainuitchildrens.com/node/29>.

Toulouse, P. *Achieving Indigenous Student Success: A Guide for Secondary Classrooms*. Winnipeg, MB: Portage
& Main Press, 2016a.

_____. *What Matters in Indigenous Education: Implementing a Vision Committed to Holism, Diversity and
Engagement*. Toronto: People for Education, 2016b.

Truth and Reconciliation Commission of Canada. (2015). *Honouring the Truth, Reconciling for the Future –
Summary of the Final Report of the Truth and Reconciliation of Canada*. Winnipeg, MB.

_____. "Residential School Locations" Retrieved from http://www.trc.ca/websites/trcinstitution/index.
php?p=12 (accessed October 18, 2017.

Wikipedia contributors, "Santa Cruz de Nuca," *Wikipedia, The Free Encyclopedia*, https://en.wikipedia.org/
w/index.php?title=Santa_Cruz_de_Nuca&oldid=801627499 (accessed October 16, 2017

Xue, K. (2013). Is There an App for That? Retrieved from <http://harvardmagazine.com/2013/11/
is-there-an-app-for-that>.

IMAGE CREDITS

Fig. 1.1: National Centre for Truth and Reconciliation Archives, Residential School Map, T00005, Truth and Reconciliation Commission of Canada

Fig. 1.2: Library and Archives Canada / PA-185530

Fig. 1.3: Canada Dept. of Indian and Northern Affairs / Library and Archives Canada / e011080269

Fig. 1.4: J.F. Moran, Library and Archives Canada, acc. no. 1973-357, a102086

Fig. 1.5: ©Art Babych

Fig. 2.1: Douglas Fast /Portage & Main Press

Fig. 2.2: *Indian Time* newspaper

Fig. 2.3, Fig. 2.4: Indigenous and Northern Affairs Canada

Fig. 2.5: The Canadian Press/Sean Kilpatrick

Fig. 3.1: Portage & Main Press

Fig. 3.2: Glenbow Archives NA-1141-10

Fig. 3.3: McCord Museum M1913

Fig. 3.4: Glenbow Archives NA-3421-10

Fig. 3.5: Glenbow Archives c230-14

Fig. 4.1: Portage & Main Press

Fig. 4.2: McCord Museum ACC2806

Fig. 4.3: McCord Museum M21019

Fig. 4.4: McCord Museum wVIEW-2031

Fig. 5.1: Drawing of the Majorville Cairn and Medicine Wheel, by John Brumley. From *Stone by Stone: Exploring Ancient Sites on the Canadian Plains*, Expanded Edition. © Liz Bryan. Heritage House Publishing, 2015. All rights reserved.